DUBAI BUSINESS LEADERS

Writer: Anna Gard
Researcher: Maxwell Preece
Book & Cover Design - David Torres Mora

Registered office
7-8 Church St, Wimborne BH21 1JH

Published by One Golden Nugget
ISBN:
978-1-7384382-0-4

CONTENTS

INTRODUCTION

In October 2021, while the world was still bruised and battered by COVID, I received an invitation to participate at the Gitex conference, the world's largest and most inclusive tech event based in Dubai. The plan was for me to interview on stage the founder of Reebok, and **One Golden Nugget's** long-time supporter, Mr Joe Foster.

Although I had previously been to Dubai on holiday, I had never conducted business in the region. So, the thought of jumping on a plane and returning to the sun-soaked city was an exciting prospect after the long and dreary lockdown.

I arrived in Dubai with hand sanitiser and medical masks at the ready, and instantly remembered why I loved the place. The city was one of the first places to come out of lockdown, and the excitement and bustle in the air was only accentuated by the eerie stillness of the rest of the world.

Driving along the Sheikh Zayed Road, I was reminded of the expansiveness of the city. The road is the longest in the region and acts as the main artery of Dubai, connecting all seven emirates. While I passed by the glistening, glass-clad, high-rise buildings, I reflected on the immense insight and visionary leadership that was transforming this former trading hub into a progressive, dynamic, multicultural city fit for the 21st century. Boasting the world's only 7-star hotel and with the second most five-star hotels in the world, Dubai's focus on tourism, luxury and tech innovation makes it a place where dreams can come true.

My interviews at Gitex with Joe Foster were a success, people loved his humble manner, humour, and English charm. It also gave me an opportunity to introduce One Golden Nugget to the people of Dubai. At that point, still in its infancy, One Golden Nugget's remit was collecting wisdom from the wise, and sharing it with the world to change lives. It's a simple concept with a profound impact, and Dubai embraced it with open arms.

With a flurry of excitement, I had one person after the next eager to share their story and how Dubai had facilitated their dream. Dubai is an ecosystem of networks, and as word got around, I was introduced to more and more people who all wanted to contribute. The energy was almost palpable.

The business leaders I met were incredibly generous when it came to introductions, and friendships were quickly formed. My idea of shining a light on the region, quickly formed; how its people did business, their mindsets, their triumphs and struggles and so 'Dubai Business Leaders' was born.

It's not just a book, but a movement to bring people together to share wisdom and empower each other. We would share personal and business stories to enlighten, educate and enthuse, whilst also supporting an educational charity through the sale of the book.

Working on Dubai Business Leaders has been an incredible experience for me, and I would like to thank each co-author, who, like Dubai itself, has helped to make a dream possible. As you read through the unique and individual journeys, lessons learned, and wisdom shared, I hope that just one of the stories will resonate with you, and change your life in one small way.

With an exceptional group of contributors, the Dubai Business Leaders' narrative reflects how Dubai has grown and developed; with vision, faith, inspiration and action. It's a city which must be celebrated as much as those business leaders who have helped build it.

Welcome to Dubai Business Leaders, Vol.1.

Steven Foster
Founder & CEO
One Golden Nugget

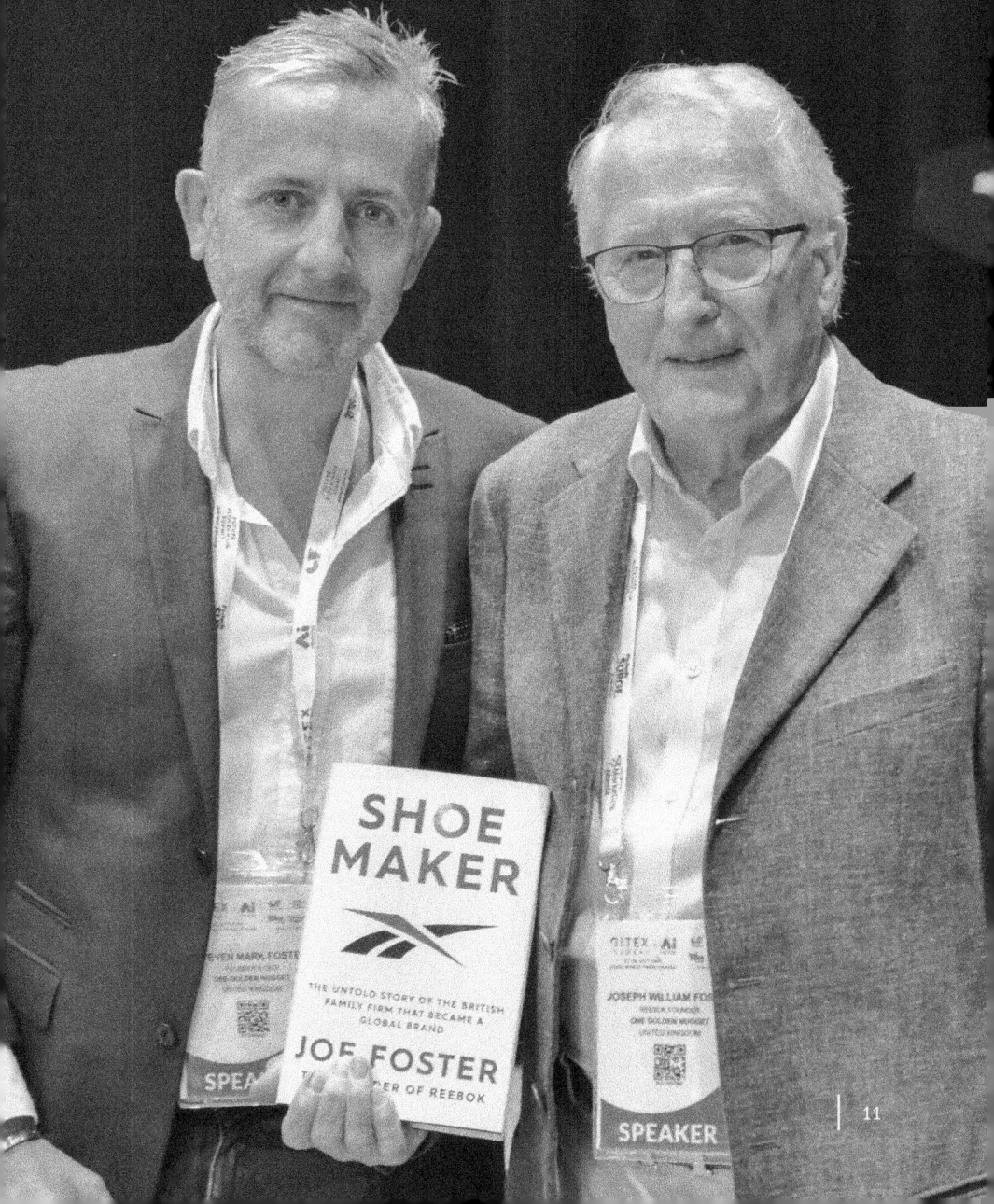

Where Dubai Business Leaders Began:
One Golden Nugget Founder, Steven Foster, with Reebok Founder, Joe Foster
at Gitex – October 2021

DARIUSH SOUDI

Founder of ARENA, Venture capitalist,
Speaker, and Philanthropist

Dariush Soudi's Instagram page feels like an oasis in a desert, with his snippets of wisdom providing inspiration and positivity on a platform often focused on vacuous content. His short and simple guidelines are a lesson on how to achieve happiness, good health, and prosperity, and he likens life to the gladiatorial arena, whereby we each fight a battle in order to live another day.

Leaving Macclesfield College with few qualifications, he's proud to have soared to the dizzy heights of entrepreneurship without a university-level education or any mentorship along the way. Now, 35 years later, he's the founder of a number of successful businesses around the world, a multi-millionaire and a sought after motivational speaker.

Dariush can truly consider himself a self made man who is more comfortable revealing his hourly rate than talking about his humanitarian and philanthropic endeavours in Thailand. As a venture capitalist, he continues to actively seek companies to invest in, sharing his knowledge and extensive experience.

Spaces for his Gladiator Mastery Programme sell out quickly as he shares his experience and knowledge about team building, sales, and networking. Promising to help people become the best version of themselves, he stops short of guaranteeing immediate financial success and abundance. As a self made man of considerable wealth, award winning entrepreneur, Marcus Aurelius fanatic, and impassioned traveller, Dariush is a key figure in the Dubai business landscape and reflects its ability to draw in crowds with the hope that some of that success and gold dust will rub off.

"NOW, DUBAI IS MY HOME, AND I CAN'T SEE MYSELF LEAVING HERE ANY TIME SOON."

HOW IT ALL STARTED

Dariush was first attracted to the world of personal development about 30 years ago after noticing that while people were repeatedly attending self improvement courses, they weren't really improving their lives in any meaningful way. He was of the opinion that these courses were really about motivation, and motivation can dwindle, resulting in people signing up for another course, creating an expensive and aimless cycle of behaviour. "It was mainly down to a lack of skills, not everyone has the charisma or personality needed to succeed, however, they can develop a skill set." With that in mind, he started teaching a simple set of skills based on the participants' own individual characters. By creating a selection of little personal nuggets, he believed their motivation would last longer.

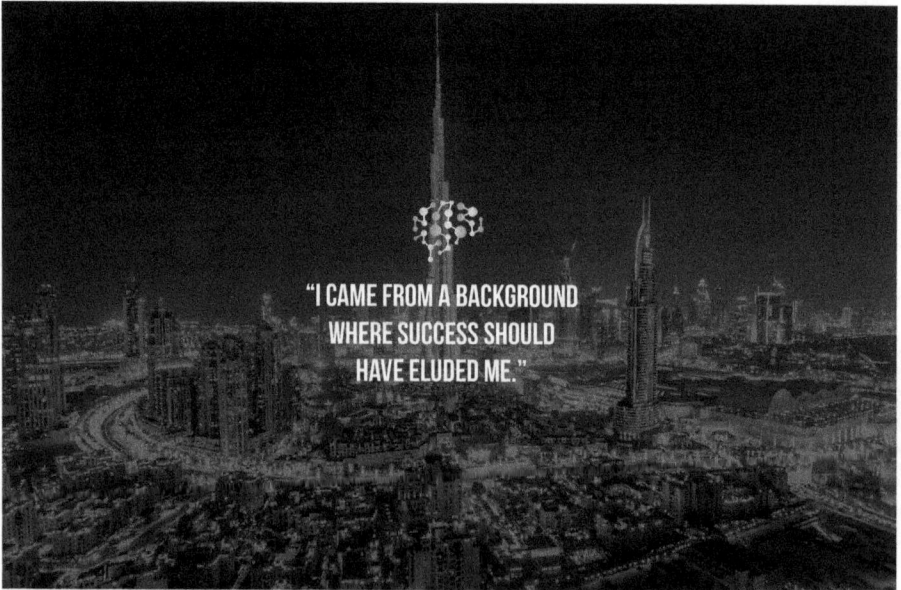

"I CAME FROM A BACKGROUND WHERE SUCCESS SHOULD HAVE ELUDED ME."

His formula has been a tremendous success, making him a millionaire many times over - even more incredible considering the seemingly insurmountable odds that were stacked against him from childhood. Because of this experience, the concept of personal development is something close to his heart. "I know how much it can change a person's outlook and prospects, and I really wanted to help others succeed as well."

MY DESTINY WAS DUBAI

Dariush's family arrived in the UK during the 1970s. As an immigrant and dyslexic, he was relentlessly bullied at school. It's perhaps not surprising that after leaving school, he couldn't keep a job, being either fired or leaving of his own accord. Nevertheless, he was quick to learn and soon realised that if you worked hard enough, you would always succeed.

His entrepreneurial spirit was sparked when he met the woman he'd eventually marry. She was in the beauty industry, and Dariush immediately spotted an opportunity in the sector. Wealth and prosperity came relatively quickly, and within 17 years, they had opened seven hugely successful health clubs.

However, a number of life-changing events occurred, which finally led Dariush to make Dubai his home. The couple divorced, and his ex-wife relocated to Dubai while he remained in the UK with their two children. When their house was broken into and he was attacked at knifepoint, he decided to send his children over to Dubai. A few weeks later, he suffered a heart attack and was told by doctors that he only had a 25% chance of survival. He explains that "this was a major wake up call, and I knew I needed to be closer to my kids, so I moved to Dubai to start a new life". He is now happily married to Angela, his second wife, and the couple share Dariush's third child together.

ds | DARIUSH SOUDI

From arriving in Dubai with less than $1000 in his pocket, Dariush now has 11 companies to his name. He loves living in Dubai, and a smile appears across his face when he talks about it, "it's like a new city, with a young administration. It's forward thinking, things happen quickly, and changes are rapid." He explains how he was captivated by an incredible sense of space and openness in the city, not to mention the blue skies and constant sunshine. A far cry from life in Manchester. For Dariush, the leadership in Dubai feels young, welcoming of change, and encouraging of growth. He reflects on his time in the UK when his Ferrari was constantly vandalised and notes that in Dubai people take pictures of his car instead because "they're inspired." Dubai is a place where Dariush feels safe and secure, the environment is "happy and optimistic", and he feels treated like a true equal.

WHAT MAKES A SUCCESSFUL LEADER?

When identifying a successful leader, Dariush is quick to point out that they never allow themselves to get too comfortable. They always have quantifiable goals with timescales to achieve them and the discipline required to make them happen.

His prescription for a successful leader is to have discipline, which is made up of 85% mindset, 10% habit keeping and 5% skill. He continues, "a successful leader needs to have discipline and strategy. As a gladiator, you need to practise every skill before you go into the arena called life. They need to ensure they are there before their competitors and also after. They need to do their admin outside of working hours, always being contactable, and making connections".

Beyond discipline, he is keen to point out that there are other elements that come together to form a successful organisation. He does a lot of work with businesses that are beginning to realise the importance of soft skills. Culture is also something he focuses on, and he believes communication is critical; not just for clients but for staff as well. When he initially goes into a business to help them achieve their goals, his first point of call is company culture. He considers the communication and respect between the directors, managers, and employees and how this trickles down to the end user. Part of the culture is having great staff, and his advice is to "hire slowly and fire fast." His experience has taught him that "successful leaders need to keep that hunger going and be prepared to make sacrifices. You have to get up early and go to bed late. Put the remote down, study, connect with people, and get out of your comfort zone."

THE IMPORTANCE OF MENTORSHIP

Most successful leaders will, at some stage, have been mentored. Dariush feels blessed to have had a range of different mentors who have helped him navigate through the many stages and challenges he has faced, including personal development, business, and spirituality. On a philosophical note, he believes that "the universe sends you the perfect mentor for each phase of your journey."

He admits that "no single mentor has ticked all the boxes", but he remembers one particular mentor who he met at the start of his career and who taught him all aspects of business; how to network, how to market himself, and how to handle clients. Later, he found a mentor who helped him overcome personal issues with mindfulness and meditation. "She helped me find inner peace, calm my mind, and connect with my spiritual side."

He clarifies that mentors aren't necessarily there for life, "as you grow and evolve, your needs and challenges will change, and different teachers will come into your life to help navigate those changes". He suggests that the key is to be open to learning from them and to trust that they have something valuable to teach.

THE FUTURE FOR BUSINESS IN DUBAI

Dariush is confident that the future of business in Dubai can be found in technology and estimates that the city will be able to "trade trillions of dollars a month" because of it. Like many astute business people, he believes that blockchain technology is the way forward, "it unleashes the world where anyone anywhere can sell their thoughts, energy, creativity, anything across the world. The global economy is just going to explode, and borders will disappear."

"BEING RICH AND SUCCESSFUL ALWAYS STARTS WITH YOUR MINDSET."

He suggests that while most of the banking sector is resisting blockchain technology, the UAE is welcoming it, "they are making huge investments in research and development in places like Israel, and I will not be surprised if, in the near future, the UAE government's trade exceeds countries like Germany and the UK." He also asserts that AI is going to be huge, using medical technology as a prime example with the introduction of tablets able to inform doctors of diagnoses and the advancement of 3D printing in Dubai.

THE FUTURE FOR DARIUSH

Dariush's childhood was fraught with instability and obstacles. He learned at a

GLADIATOR
MASTERY

"MANY OF THE PEOPLE I COACH ARE ADULTS, AND THEY'VE HAD NEGATIVITY AND LIMITING BELIEF SYSTEMS DRILLED INTO THEM BY THEIR UPBRINGING. SO I AM NOW CREATING A PROGRAM CALLED JUNIOR GLADIATORS. WE WANT TO TRY AND BRING OPTIMISM AND ENERGY INTO CHILDREN'S LIVES."

very young age that "life is not guaranteed" after losing his father when he was only three and a half years old and then losing his grandfather, who died in front of him when he was just seven.

During a trip to Iran for his grandmother's funeral 20 years ago, he visited a city where his grandfather was a former mayor. As a small group of people started to gather around him to pay their respects, he became moved with emotion. This public show of respect completely changed his perspective, and he began to think about his legacy. "It really made me think about what I'm going to leave behind, and after that experience, I started to post regular messages on social media promoting my values and thoughts." With over 1 million followers, he's now writing a book to inspire and encourage others to succeed.

He doesn't believe his ability to inspire should be limited to adults either, explaining how he's developing an offshoot of his gladiator masterclasses. "A lot of the people I coach are adults, and they've had negativity and limiting belief systems drilled into them by their upbringing. So I am now creating a programme called Junior Gladiators. We want to try and bring optimism and energy into children's lives, and positive energy towards money." His dissatisfaction with the education system is clear, and he explains that financial literacy should be a priority in schools to "show children how their lives can be limitless." He questions why "1% of the

world controls 99% of the wealth", believing that there's enough to go around. "Just because I have it, doesn't mean that someone else can't have it as well. Wealth is a good thing, it can help good people do good things".

As a savvy business person, Dariush is aware that he earns more money in the US than he does in the UAE, so he envisages his long term future hopping back and forth. Yet the UAE has set such a high bar for quality of life and standards of living that nowhere else can even compare. He clarifies, "Emirates Airlines are exceptional, and the hotels in Dubai make 5 star hotels in Las Vegas look like 2 stars. You tend to get spoiled, as nothing in the world can match the exacting standards here. For me, Dubai is home, I can't see me leaving it long term."

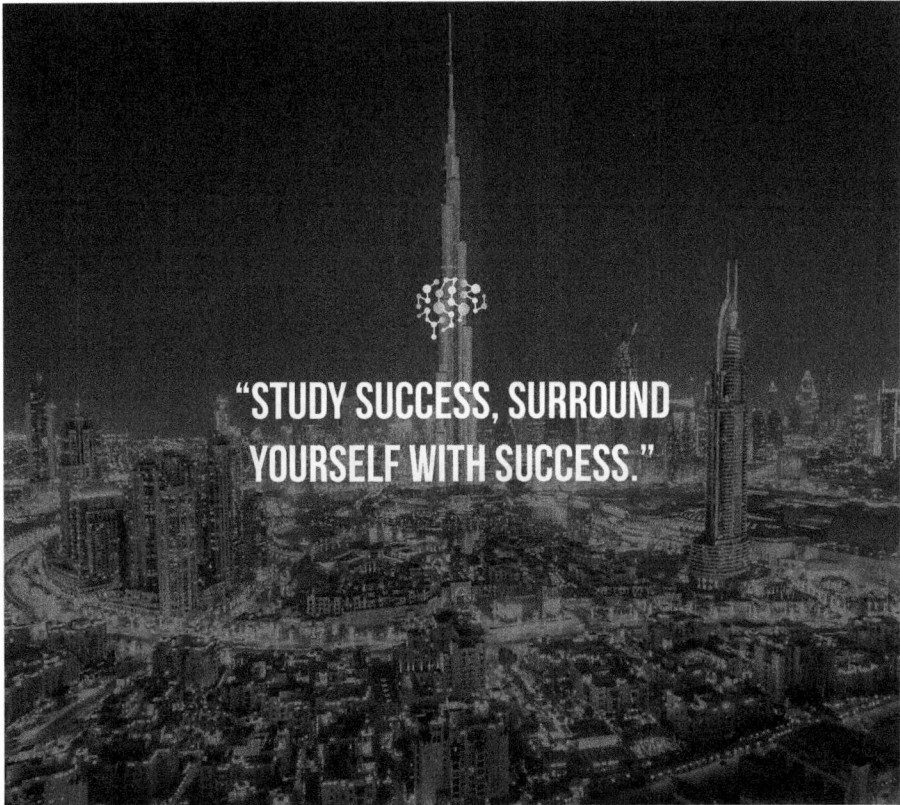

"STUDY SUCCESS, SURROUND YOURSELF WITH SUCCESS."

DUBAI
BUSINESS
LEADERS

ds | DARIUSH SOUDI

LUCY CHOW

Women of the Future Top 100
Arabian Business 50 Inspiring Women Leaders 2023,
Women in Games Ambassador, Board Advisor, Futurist Investor,
Video Host, Global Speaker, International Author

C onsidering herself a "friend of the new", Lucy Chow's recent book *Changing the Game* explores how video games are redefining business and education for the next generation. Having lived in Dubai for 17 years, she is certainly no stranger to trends and developments in the business world and has become an expert in Tech-Diplomacy, Web 3.0, the metaverse, and digital transformation. One of the OG angel investors and an original founding member of the private members' organisation 'The Capital Club', Lucy has played an integral part in transforming Dubai into a hub for business and innovation. She has an impressive number of accolades to her name, having been recognised by Arabian Business as one of the 50 female business leaders in 2023, voted one of Titanium Magazine's Top 50 Global Inspirational Women to Look Out for in 2022, one of HSBC's 75 Faces of the UAE, one of #LinkedInTopVoices for MENA and Top100 Women of The Future.

Lucy took her first international flight from Canada at the age of 25, travelling to China, Hong Kong, and New York before eventually settling in Dubai with her husband. It was a significant move, which gave Lucy the space to thrive in a small but rapidly expanding business community. When they first arrived, the population of Dubai was only 1.5 million, today, that number has reached 3.5 million. Despite this surge in growth, Lucy explains that the city still feels small enough so that you don't get obscured, "to be recognised as a business leader, an entrepreneur, a thought leader, and an author - I would have been lost in most cities." She explains that Dubai has the

"TO ENSURE A FULL LIFE, GIVE SOMETHING BACK TO THE COMMUNITY YOU'RE PART OF - IT DOESN'T HAVE TO BE MONEY, IT COULD JUST BE YOUR TIME AND SUPPORT."

unique ability to "tap into a lot of geographies and expand quickly." It's this unusual mix of localism and globalism that offers people the perfect platform to showcase their talents.

As a former banker with knowledge and experience of events, she was able to identify what was missing and what needed to be improved. She felt there was an appetite out there "for more activations," prompting Lucy to start her events management company, The Elements Group, which now has a strong reputation for its focus on fundraising and philanthropy.

Lucy's prominence in Dubai has offered her a valuable seat at the table, and she's excited to be part of the city's future. Beyond being one of the safest places to live in the world, it's also set to be "one of the top metaverse centres in the world." And, having recently read the Dubai Future Foundation's 'Future Opportunities Report', Lucy suggests that there is currently an atmosphere of innovation and excitement that is attracting even more new businesses on a daily basis.

CHANGING THE GAME

Lucy's book *Changing the Game* aims to dispel the outdated view of video games as a mindless, counter-educational activity, exploring their transformative potential to "allow deeper connections with our world and create greater cultural understanding." As a case in point, she reveals a whole new world of "good games." The book shines a light on collaborative games that develop leadership skills, games where you can learn another language, educational games, and ambient games.

Perhaps surprisingly, the statistics show that "esports is bigger than the film industry, the music industry, and the sports industry combined." Esports tournaments are held in every corner of the globe and broadcast to millions, with professional players, teams, and lucrative sponsorship deals. Her book taps into a robust and thriving industry overflowing with investment opportunities, emerging and diverse career paths, and innovation potential.

Lucy was introduced to the world of esports by her son, but she was inspired to write *Changing the Game* after attending a number of conferences. Listening to a wide range of speakers from around the globe talk about the sector inspired her. The result is a compilation of 34 essays from thought-leaders within the multibillion-dollar industry, united in the aim of changing the narrative around gaming and bringing it to the forefront.

While she was initially drawn into the world of gaming because of her son's enthusiasm, she is aware that it's not just the youth that have caught the gaming bug. Lucy's parents, now in their eighties, happily compete against each other playing games on their mobile phones, and evidence suggests it can even keep dementia at bay. Surgeons and pilots use computer games as part of their training, they are now a staple educational tool used in schools, and people turned to gaming during COVID to feel less isolated or bored. With the "technological innovation of AI and virtual reality, it's become this immersive experience that's just going to get better." Lucy's prediction is that there will soon be esports hotels opening up, perhaps first in the Middle East and North Africa region.

However, despite the injection of life-like graphics into gameplay, Lucy suggests that this advancement in technology has actually influenced a return to more nostalgic formats, noticing "a revival of older games where it's pixelated because there's a comfort in it."

WOMEN AND WORK

As an Ambassador for Women in Games, Lucy has a strong interest in advocating for more women in the gaming industry. Conscious that only 15 years ago, women made up 6% of the industry workforce, she's very keen to share her wisdom. "Let go of that self-doubt and think about how you can enter the industry strategically, and focus on what makes you unique. Go on to LinkedIn and start reaching out to people doing what *you* want to be doing, build up your social capital, that is key." She also specifies the importance of mentorship. As a young recruit at HSBC, Lucy recalls feeling too intimidated to approach board level members of staff. Looking back, she believes her life would have taken a different turn if she had just had the confidence to reach out.

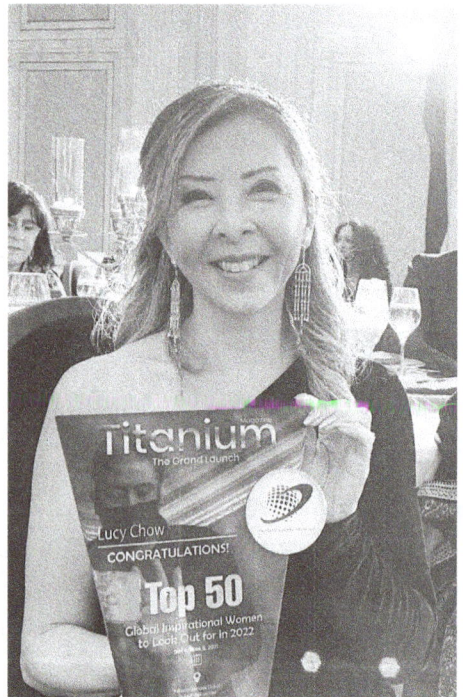

Now a successful businesswoman in her own right, she implores ambitious young people to take a leap of faith and find their champion, regardless of the industry they choose.

A patron of female entrepreneurs, Lucy is keen to highlight that women starting out usually have lower levels of capitalisation, using about a third of the debt finance than their male counterparts and being less likely to use private equity or venture capital. Yet despite the odds, "female-founded firms still outperform firms with all male founder teams." She suggests that women building businesses need access to smart finance, need to see more visible success stories, and be able to facilitate connections by increasing their entry into global business networks. An area she specifically focuses on is encouraging more women to become investors via #2022FemaleAngels. "One way to guarantee more funding is given to female entrepreneurs is to ensure the people making the funding decision on the other side of the table are women." Considering that women make 85% of consumer decisions and approximately 50% of tech consumer decisions, it makes sense to level the playing field.

MENTAL HEALTH AND WELLBEING

Lucy is refreshingly candid when discussing the stresses of corporate life, and reflects on the impact of a particularly "toxic work environment" during her first role. A circumstance that eventually led to her being laid off could have caused irreparable damage to her confidence as a young, entry-level employee. But she reminded herself that her job was not her identity; she had a supportive and loving husband and a solid set of true friends, which allowed her to overcome setbacks and move forward. "Having a strong support network and identity outside of my work really grounded me."

A big component of wellbeing and managing mental health is remembering to allocate time for yourself. She recalls an analogy she heard a long time ago that still resonates, "think about your energy stores as pebbles in a jar, every time you go out, your pebbles come out of the jar, so you have to find time to make sure you're putting the pebbles back in." For Lucy, activities that help her put those pebbles back in the jar include a mixture of yoga, Zumba, or Body Balance. She also makes sure to "ring-fence" her weekends as a time for friends, family, and re-energising.

"FOR PEOPLE NAVIGATING THE CORPORATE WORLD, MAKE SURE YOU HAVE A SPONSOR."

EDUCATION

Previously, as a Board Director of Little Thinking Minds, an award-winning children's education company, and a non-executive director of the charity Educate Girls Globally, teaching and learning have always been important topics for Lucy. "I am super passionate about getting entrepreneurial skills taught in schools." Beyond that, she is currently excited to be a board trustee with the American School in Dubai, chairing the Facilities Committee in the fit out of a "Design and Innovation Centre," something she believes will "greatly impact the trajectory of our curriculum to meet the needs of the future."

As part of her passion for creating social impact through education, she recommends Julia Freeland's book, Who You Know, which promotes networking as a necessary tool for elevation in life and work. With a particular focus on underprivileged school children, the book advocates for a school-based LinkedIn system that can "expand their world and make connections, even being encouraged to apply to university or an apprenticeship."

DOWN TO BUSINESS

"Share everything you know," is a rule Lucy keenly repeats and demonstrates in

her desire to develop and improve. Among her many talents, Lucy presents her own video series targeted at entrepreneurs and shares valuable wisdom and experience, not only from her own perspective but also from guests appearing on her show. Some of her practical tips for procuring investment are:

1. Don't be too precious when sharing your idea, as the VC community is built on trust.

2. You should be looking for partners who can give you references and testimonials.

3. Potential investors will ask to see a roadmap to show where you are at, and, more importantly, where you are headed.

3. Be ready to share your Sales/Branding/Marketing pitch deck - investors want to understand the founders' thinking process.

"NEVER STOP BEING CURIOUS, CONTINUE TO BE A FRIEND TO THE NEW."

mastercard.

"My philosophy in terms of how
I approach marketing is to test,
learn, optimise and scale."

HAYSAM FAHMY

VICE PRESIDENT AND HEAD OF
MARKETING SERVICES AT MASTERCARD
MIDDLE EAST, AFRICA & EASTERN
EUROPE - MASTERCARD

FOUR NUGGETS FOR LIFE

BE DISCIPLINED TO YOUR PASSION

Listen to your own sense of what you love doing and then be disciplined in figuring out how you can be more curious, evolve, grow and learn. Use that as an area to play as opposed to work and forget the noise from random people telling you what you should do.

GOALS

Really understand what it is that you absolutely love doing and build goals around that. To improve on the thing that you are passionate about, set high ambitious goals, but be incremental in the way you achieve them, and assume that nothing is in your way.

OVERCOME YOUR EGO

We do things because of how we were raised, and that gets programmed into us, affecting the way we operate. Some habits are good for achieving your goals, but some hold you back. Identify them, tackle them and ask for feedback from those close to you, which means overcoming your ego.

HAVE AN OPEN MINDSET

Experimentation in work, play and in life is critical. So have a mindset that is open to achieving goals in different ways. Be open to trying different things and don't be comfortable using just one tool or one way of working. Experiment, learn, grow.

CHRIS WRIGHT

CEO of The Wright Group

O riginally from Liverpool, Chris Wright (known colloquially as 'The Party King') has almost single-handedly transformed the reputation of Dubai. Initially, the thriving metropolis may have been considered a preserve for the elite, with their Ferraris, Rolexes, and Armani suits. Now, Chris is helping to evolve the city's image as the heart of global entertainment for all.

His journey to entrepreneurship began as a DJ in both the UK and Ibiza. Already drawing large crowds in Europe, he decided to try Dubai and showed up with nothing but a suitcase, boundless energy, and a far-reaching imagination. A decade later, he's made a name for himself as a savvy businessman, an events guru, and the founder of several thriving businesses within the hospitality industry.

With a Degree in Marketing, Chris has won a number of awards for his ability to create spaces for community, whether that's somewhere for fun and partying until the early hours, or just a place to mingle and network - there's something for everyone at every hour. From a Seven Deadly Sins show extravaganza to a low-key expat brunch, his events are famous and attract thousands of paying guests.

Chris comes across as amiable, informal, and down to earth, yet his business acumen is sharp, precise, and well considered. Although he frequently rubs shoulders with A-list celebrities, he remains steadfast that no matter who you are, everyone should be

"HAVING A STRONG MINDSET AND BEING PREPARED FOR THE WORST IS ESSENTIAL IN BUSINESS."

treated with equal respect. As a man who, in his 30s, has already achieved great wealth and success, Chris is surprisingly unassuming and humble - a rare combination in his business.

Since settling in Dubai, he's progressed rapidly and is now the go-to for event planning across the board. Ladies day pool parties, family brunches, club nights and dinner parties are only the tip of the iceberg. He's one of the top hospitality consultants in the game, creating concepts from scratch for brands such as Jumeirah, building a venue from the ground up to launching it onto the market and making it award-winning. One of his latest projects has become a signature hot-spot on the Dubai nightlife scene, Mi Amie is an outdoor rooftop restaurant/ bar concept with stunning views of the Museum of the Future, named the most beautiful building in the world.

Money doesn't seem to be his main motivation, he's a man with a mission; to do business well, to have fun doing it, and to bring people together. A number of his events have also raised money for worthwhile charities. He hosts around 1600 events each year, with an astounding 5000 guests in attendance on a weekly basis. While he no longer has the time to focus on his passion for DJ-ing, for the moment, he's enjoying seeing how much value he's able to bring to local communities through his entrepreneurial endeavours.

WHY DUBAI?

Chris first visited Dubai as a young 16-year-old, and specifies how much it's changed since then. He recalls visiting an exhibition and seeing models of the buildings they were planning to construct, like the 5-star hotels and glass clad skyscrapers. As a teenager, all this seemed really exciting, and he couldn't wait to return and be part of it as an adult.

At 23, he made the big move with only £2000 in his bank account and nowhere to live. Now, just over 10 years later, he generates over $100m revenue for his clients. He summarises, "what I have done is basically create trends and concepts to increase tourism in one of the most expensive places in the world." Working with world-renowned establishments like Atlantis The Palm, he's been able to connect luxury venues with the wider public for all to enjoy.

For Chris, Dubai's reputation on a global scale is changing rapidly. People still view it as opulent, but it's now seen more widely as modern, safe, and an enjoyable place to come and visit, work, or live. One of the many highlights for him is "the fact that it's tolerant of all backgrounds, it's a welcoming place." For work, it's the perfect place because "there's hardly any crime, people respect each other, it's well monitored, and you can do business securely because of the culture that has been developed."

HOSPITALITY IN DUBAI

The Wright Group is a holding company with a number of complementary companies, all under the umbrella of hospitality. One of his companies aims to boost tourism and travel in Dubai, working with influencers and celebrities to promote the city as a destination hot-spot. Another business is an entertainment agency that recruits international talent to work in some of Dubai's biggest hotels like the Armani hotel at the Burj Khalifa to FIVE hotels and resorts.

Beyond this, his passion is corporate and non-corporate event planning, which he takes from concept, development, and brand creation all the way through to ensuring seats are filled. If a fashion brand wants to generate hype for a new flagship store opening in Dubai, he has a separate marketing agency to do all the artwork, graphic design, and content creation for PR, flying in influencers and celebrities to endorse the brand and their products. He also manages marketing campaigns, producing, directing, and editing promotional videos for the events, and works closely with influencers to market their own personal brands, using Dubai as a shiny backdrop.

While this may seem like a lot for one man, all of his companies really work in harmony to create an empire of hospitality services, and by operating on the ground, he's able to utilise his connections to their full potential. Alongside access to locations, hotels, and venues, he has a wide network that puts him in a unique position to "organise pretty much anything in Dubai." His advice to others is to "believe in the opportunities that this particular industry gives you, especially in Dubai, the sky's the limit."

DUBAI: THE DESTINATION FOR THRIVING BUSINESS

Dubai is all about hospitality. Unlike most destinations across the globe, where tourists visit on a seasonal basis, in Dubai, it's all year round. He specifies that one of the most popular concepts he developed was for tourists to be able to access Dubai in 7 days and 7 nights, something he suggests wouldn't necessarily work for other destinations. He created an itinerary complete with both daytime and nighttime activities for tourists to really get the full Dubai experience. For him, affordability was a key ingredient - Dubai

is notoriously expensive, but he's managed to work with some of the most high-end venues to market their less busy periods and create a more economical experience. It increases their revenue, but it also gives them extra exposure.

Chris is certain that part of the reason he's been able to achieve such success in Dubai is because he thinks outside the box. The Family Brunch Dubai targets a different audience to open up the marketplace even wider. Catering specifically to families, they even have on-site nannies, offering an alternative experience to the parties, clubs, and 7-star hotels that we've come to associate with Dubai.

He refuses to get complacent. The city is so fast-paced, and it's crucial to have a strong team that can cover all bases 24 hours a day. Chris has around 25 full-time staff members and prioritises having a diverse group of people around him to support business operations.

As one of the most visited destinations worldwide, it's a very multicultural community, generating traction from all sectors. According to Chris, it's a great place to meet different people, especially in hotel resorts, so he's managed to gain a lot of celebrity contacts through events. Normally, he'd have to go through their PA, but he's found that it's much easier to talk to them if they're staying at the hotel, as they're in 'holiday mode' and more open to chatting. Plus, if he makes sure they have a great time, he's more likely to get an opportunity to work with them again. For someone in Chris's business, these networking opportunities are second to none.

ADVICE FOR ASPIRING ENTREPRENEURS

Chris' key to successfully setting up a new business is carefully calculated projections. Additional and unanticipated costs can often crop up and accumulate over the process of building a business, so accurate budgeting, thorough research, and getting advice from similar business owners can help mitigate any potential roadblocks. Due diligence within the hiring process is crucial; get background checks done and follow up on references. This is particularly important in Dubai, as you have to immediately pay for visas and medical insurance once you hire someone, so you want to be sure about the people you choose. For Chris, treating everyone with respect, whether that be a client, employee, or anyone in between, is of the utmost importance because you never know what someone's gone through or is perhaps going through.

Chris has a bank of practical advice for budding entrepreneurs, and he's more than happy to share it. He starts with, "resist the desire to spend every dime." Always set aside a percentage of profits each month for contingencies. Be mindful of the environmental impact of your business, "this will mitigate any backlash from consumers and could contribute to long-term business viability." Be prepared for rejection and betrayal. Rejection can impact your confidence in your own brand, but it also provides an opportunity to learn from others' perspectives. Be aware that betrayal can occur even in your inner circle. "While many people may initially seem positive and loyal, not everyone has good intentions. Some may take advantage of your success and act in their own self-interest." Lastly, a business venture can be overwhelming and take up all your time and energy, so don't forget your friends and family.

"Bring ideas to the table, be passionate, and put a smile on your face every single day, even if you're having a rough day. It's all about positivity and believing in yourself, because that can change your life one day."

Manifest your progress by following these simple actions:

• *Put down on paper what you want to achieve in 1 year, 5 years, and 10 years.*
• *Read it every morning, so you are constantly reminding yourself of your goals.*
• *You need an end goal to keep you on the right path - an action plan from A-Z.*

EFFECTIVE LEADERSHIP

Chris is a naturally approachable individual who extends that accessibility into his leadership behaviours. "I will always have a shot with the staff if we've had a great night, and they enjoy the fact that I will celebrate with them." He extends this sometimes by having dinner together so that he can sit down with them and have a proper conversation. "I think as a business leader, it is really important to be approachable with employees, so they feel they can speak to you about their problems, aspirations, and dreams. He likes to know what their personal goals are, whether they want to buy a car, a house, or if they are looking to start a family, "because if I can help them achieve what they want, through changing the structure of their pay to a commission, giving them a side hustle project, or offering them more hours to boost earnings, then I want to be able to offer them those alternatives so that they don't feel that things can never change." For Chris, being an effective leader is about "giving your team the empowerment to be able to change their everyday lives and what they're doing."

IT'S ALL IN YOUR HEAD

Chris recommends reading 'It's All in Your Head' by musician Russ. "It has helped me understand the immense value of self-belief in my journey towards success. It has taught me that self-doubt can be detrimental, as our thoughts can consume us and lead us down the wrong path. I learned the power of truly believing in myself and my abilities. It has given me the strength to persevere through challenging times when others might have given up. I have proven to myself that I can start and manage multiple businesses, invest in various projects, and continuously grow my ventures,

even in industries where I initially had limited knowledge. This newfound belief in my capabilities has been a game-changer, allowing me to pursue and achieve success in areas I never thought possible."

THE FUTURE OF ENTERTAINMENT: 10 YEARS TIME

Chris believes that due to recent international brand investment in the area, Dubai will soon be the number one destination for global entertainment. Big name artists are consistently choosing to perform in Dubai, high-end and celebrity chefs are gravitating towards restaurants, and customer service is exceptional. Overall, staff go above and beyond to create a luxurious and unforgettable experience. To capitalise on this exponential growth, Chris's personal goal for the next ten years is to open his own hotel or be a partner in a resort in order to "expand on [his] business model and provide an unrivalled hospitality experience to a wider audience."

DUBAI
BUSINESS
LEADERS

"When working collaborative, It's important to create a safe space, and create an opportunity for the other to shine, to own the initiative and bring the work forward."

Alfredo Cramerotti
Art Curator

"Be bold enough to take calculated risks while you are still young, and failure is OK, you just need to figure out what went wrong and how to get it right."

Priven Reddy
CEO - Various tech companies

"The power of working collaborative allows you
to be driven, efficient and motivated all the time.
There is always support and energy, and if one has
to tackle things outside their comfort zone, the
other brings their skills and wisdom."

Auronda Scalera
Art Curator

"The universe has a plan, there are things that are put in our
way for us to overcome, there are opportunities that present
themselves, and things happen for a reason."

Philip Wride
Creator - Chained to Champion

MAHMOUD BARTAWI

Board Member, C-Level Executive, Entrepreneur

Affter a decade working in the banking sector, Mahmoud took a courageous leap of faith after noticing a gap in the food and beverage industry, and started his journey into entrepreneurship. His mission was to create a chain of healthy food brands and his first company, UNDER500, flourished into a network of 26 active kitchens in Dubai, Kuwait, Saudi Arabia, the UK and the USA, before it was acquired by KITOPI. Since then, Mahmoud has continued to innovate, creating numerous health-focused food brands, whilst engaging in franchise sales, negotiations, and acquisitions.

Having left behind a comfortable and secure job to pursue entrepreneurship, Mahmoud has gained valuable insights that make him an ideal advisor for those wishing to leave behind their traditional 9-5 routine for a leap into the unknown. He recommends easing in gently with a side hustle, whilst still maintaining a regular salary from a day job, emphasising the significance of a consistent monthly income. For Mahmoud, the ability to cope without a fixed salary is the most crucial factor to consider when venturing into the realm of entrepreneurship.

Throughout his entrepreneurial journey, Mahmoud has learned invaluable lessons that have enabled him to navigate the challenges and opportunities that have arisen along the way. Having received his education from an American school in Dubai, he broadened his horizons by spending a year in a Texas high school, offering him a multicultural perspective. He also had the benefit of a longstanding connection with

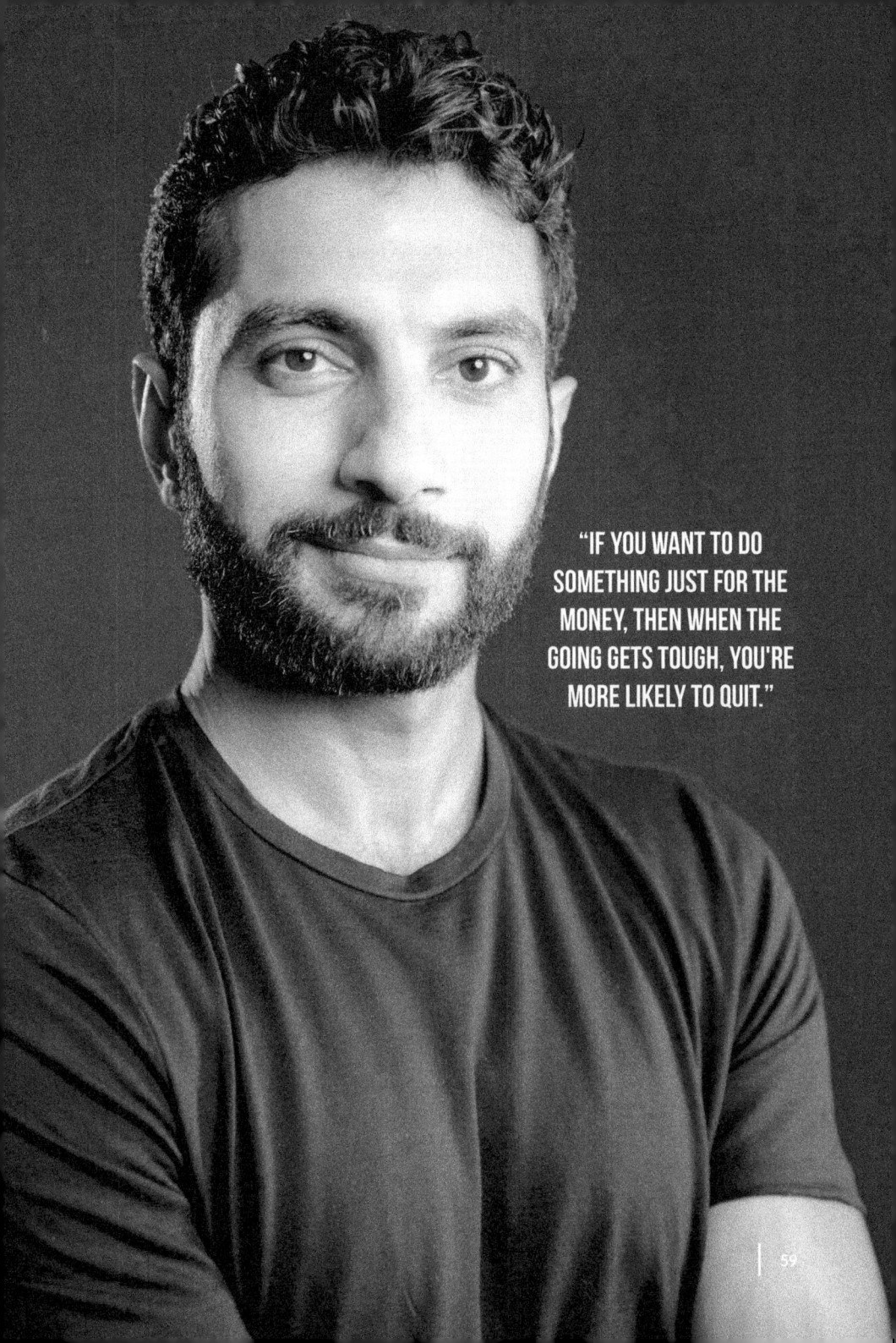

"IF YOU WANT TO DO SOMETHING JUST FOR THE MONEY, THEN WHEN THE GOING GETS TOUGH, YOU'RE MORE LIKELY TO QUIT."

his English teacher Robert Lawless, who tutored him for ten years and gave him an invaluable piece of advice; when you are faced with a huge, seemingly insurmountable task, break it down into smaller chunks, and it will become more manageable. It's a habit he still adopts today, enabling him to not only "think outside the box" but put these ideas to action. Having his father as an entrepreneurial role model, someone who "started from nothing," was an exceptional asset for Mahmoud, who admired the concept of starting something from scratch. He explains, "at home, I wouldn't see a fixed pay and would see the struggles my dad had, but, as a kid, I enjoyed it, I thought it was all very interesting."

Despite his early interest in entrepreneurship, Mahmoud studied for a degree in accounting and finance and went to work in a bank. It was the rigidity of policy and procedure which made him think again about his professional future. He was dynamic, with a growth mindset, and started to question the corporate barriers put in place which stopped him from attempting to find a better way of doing things. He also started to develop an oeuvre of an idea based on the concept of healthy eating, which was to become his passion.

YOU ARE WHAT YOU EAT

Mahmoud remembers the early morning walks along the beach with his father who, from an early age, taught him about the importance of food and nutrition and how almost every ailment has a cure in nature. Mahmoud explains that a decade ago in Dubai "healthy foods sounded very uncool," it had the reputation of being bland and unimaginative. However, he wanted to share nutritional information and help people living in Dubai to get fit and healthy, and had a few ideas of how he could get things started. He knew of a health food restaurant near to where he lived and approached them with a franchise offer. However, at the age of 27, Mahmoud faced his first major rejection, as the restaurant owner declined his proposal.

Nevertheless, Mahmoud refused to let this hold him back. His patience and persistence paid off, and he moved towards more exciting things, demonstrating an ability to think outside the box, problem solve and pivot. Without any experience in the restaurant business, he bought a "non-healthy" franchise, ran it for a year and then sold it back to the original owner at cost. He didn't need financial profit, what he needed was first-hand experience of the industry, that was invaluable.

As a strategic thinker, one of Mahmoud's strengths is being acutely aware of the importance of good collaboration, and he found a strong alliance in Fadi Ghaly, the co-founder of UNDER500. At first, the company name might seem curious for a health food business, but it developed from a calculation the co-founders made that the "average burn of an individual is 1800 calories, so they developed dishes which came below that number. Thereby guaranteeing weight loss if customers ate their calorie controlled meals three times a day."

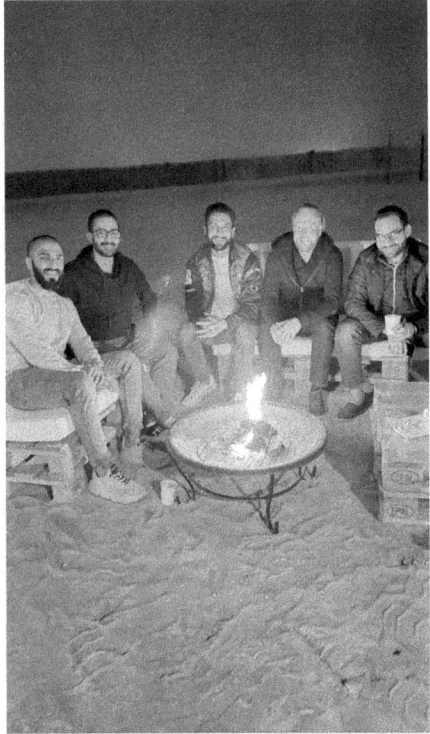

Given Mahmoud's expertise around health and fitness, he has a strong aversion to fast food establishments that offer highly processed meals lacking in essential nutrients, claiming that these types of foods can become addictive. The World Obesity Atlas 2022 predicts that by 2030, the number of people grappling with obesity will reach a staggering one billion. To combat this startling projection, Mahmoud's business model aims to make a meaningful impact by providing a convenient way to manage calorie intake and achieve weight loss goals.

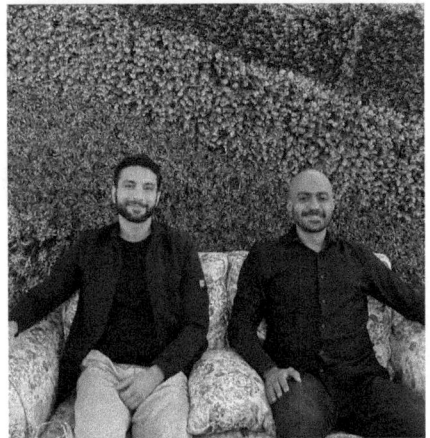

Although his business focus is on healthy eating, he also believes wholeheartedly in the many benefits of regular exercise. "As a human being, you need to get out once a day, find something you enjoy. If you want to talk on the phone with your friends, why not go for a walk with them

somewhere, go towards sporty activities, so you can build that social element." He also suggests that laughter is a good way to release endorphins and believes that people who take care of their bodies are taken "a little bit more seriously….it shows that you care."

A firm believer in "you are what you eat," Mahmoud warns against fad diets, suggesting the only "scientific" method of losing weight is calorie intake minus exercise. This may be a simple equation, but Mahmoud still needed to "convince people that healthy food was the scientific way to do it," as the promise of rapid weight loss from fad diets was alluring. Nevertheless, statistics indicate that crash diets are largely unsustainable and instead, Mahmoud proposes the use of online calorie calculators for more long-lasting weight loss. "AI can tell you how long it would take to lose weight, depending on your calorie intake."

EFFECTIVE LEADERSHIP

For Mahmoud, being an effective leader means being able to make decisions, "it doesn't matter if your decision is right or wrong, it's the ability to make a decision." As a modern-day businessman and progressive thinker, sustainability is a decision he must be continually aware of. A healthy body cannot exist without a healthy planet, but Mahmoud accepts that most things in the UAE are imported. He insists that it's about time that societies started "trying to do things at home. You save on the carbon footprint [and] everything sourced locally is excellent." He's obviously looking ahead for several reasons, citing the possibility of using hydroponic farms to be "self-sufficient...especially with so many variables."

SETTING UP IN DUBAI

Having already launched two businesses from scratch, Mahmoud suggests that "Dubai is one of the easiest places in the world to set up a business." He has other countries to compare to, explaining that when he took "UNDER500 to five different countries, it wasn't as easy as Dubai." Despite being an Emirati, he's adamant that he's not biased when he claims that "people love to live in Dubai, they aspire to attach this amazing brand name to themselves." The fact that his co-founders were Egyptian and English also made no difference in Dubai. He explains that "Dubai has made it really easy for people to partner up... There's a lot of coworking space, you can meet interesting people, and you get value."

ROUTE TO MARKET TACTICS AND STRATEGIES

Keen to discuss the complexities of business strategies, Mahmoud advises that anyone looking to grow their business in Dubai has a distinct advantage, as they can also put Saudi Arabia on their pitch deck. "Most investors are looking for growth in Saudi Arabia and Dubai as a model to prove your business." He continues, "Dubai is also an easier place to attract talent. People love to live in Dubai, so [it's] a great place to start your brand and position it for Saudi Arabia. When people invest in you, they invest in acquiring the Saudi market." His enthusiasm for Dubai is infectious as he states, "it's a really cool place to live, a really cool place to meet talent."

Saudi Arabia is not too far off his radar, as he claims that the average age in the country is just 27, with many of the population under that age. He can see potential profits to be made, and proposes that Dubai should be used as a starting base for companies to scale to the rest of the world, starting with Saudi Arabia.

Mahmoud is a diligent and shrewd businessman, observant of potential gaps in the market and an enjoyer of the thrill and excitement of a start-up environment. He is also a collaborator, seeking partnerships to continually improve, and believes that co-founded enterprises are "really important." He sees strength in someone knowing what they are good at and then finding others to fill any weaknesses. His final advice to those wishing to follow in his footsteps is, "you need to humble yourself to know that you can't do it by yourself [because] if anyone tells you they can do it by themselves, they are still learning."

"FOR YOU TO REALLY
SUCCEED, IT NEEDS TO BE
FOR SOMETHING MORE
THAN THE MONEY."

"YOUR BODY IS THE MOST IMPORTANT
THING THAT YOU HAVE. IT'S VERY HARD
TO THINK WELL WHEN YOUR BODY IS
NOT IN A GOOD SHAPE."

DR MARIAM SHAIKH

Founder and CEO
of MS Education Consultants FZ LLC

H

aving been brought up in Mumbai, India, Dr Mariam Shaikh has now been part of the UAE educational landscape for an impressive 38 years. Making her start as the owner of a preschool, she then became Head Principal of a number of K-12 schools, before moving into recruitment, marketing and student experience as a Senior Leader and Vice President for "some of the largest and most-reputed universities in the UAE."

As a lifelong advocate for education and founder of MS Education Consultants, Dr Shaikh's passion is clearly embedded within educational and mentoring schemes. She also strongly believes in active participation in public forums and expanding her network. She has had numerous accolades awarded to her, including, Global Excellence in Education 2021 from H.E Sheikh Eng. Salem Bin Sultan Al Qasimi, the Prestigious Fame Times International Excellence Award 2021, Outstanding Contribution to the Education Industry Under the Patronage of The Private Office of H.E Sheikh Ahmed Bin Faisal Al-Qassimi 2021, Entrepreneur Award Winner - Emirates Women Award 2022 from H.H. Sheikh Ahmed Bin Saeed Al Maktoum, 100 Women Power Leaders 2023 by White Page International UK and Lifetime Achievement Award 2020 from the International Inspirational Women.

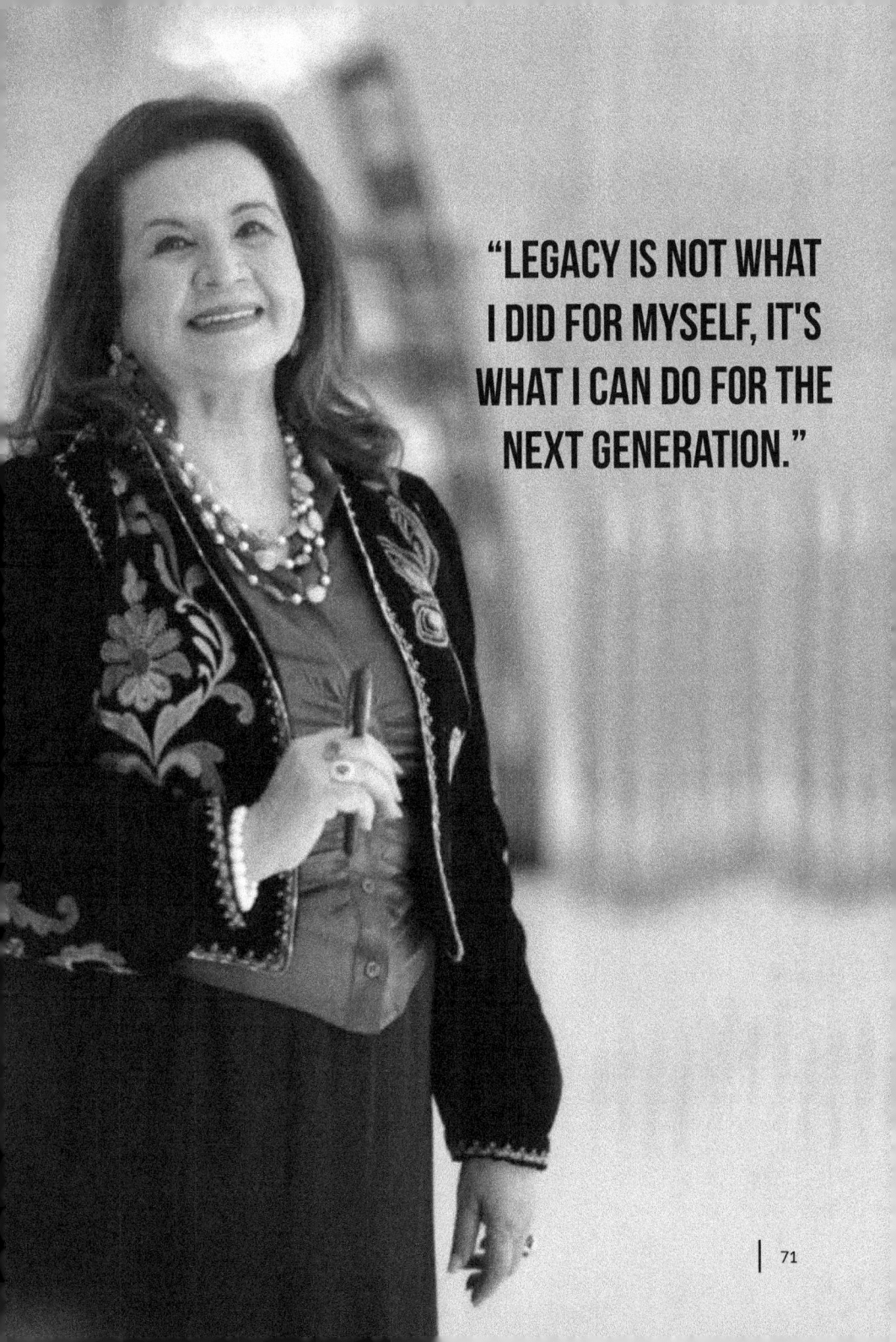

"LEGACY IS NOT WHAT I DID FOR MYSELF, IT'S WHAT I CAN DO FOR THE NEXT GENERATION."

Having directly contributed to the exponential growth of the student population in Dubai educational establishments, such as the Canadian University, Amity University and Heriot-Watt University Dubai Campus, Dr Shaikh moved forward with her own venture, supporting students with university admissions, providing education consulting, organising student cultural exchange programmes and offering online training. MS Education Consultants started in 2020 and reached a milestone in 2022, when her enterprise was appointed the official 'Middle East Strategist' for the University of Guelph in Ontario, Canada.

STUDENT WELLBEING AND ENGAGEMENT

During her tenure as the Vice President of International Partnerships at a university, Dr Shaikh took the initiative to establish and execute multiple MOUs with institutions in the United States, Austria, India, and China. Her goal was to promote internationalization and foster cross-cultural student mobility. Notably, she played a pivotal role in pioneering the enrolment of 120 Chinese students in Dubai.

Driven by her mission to empower students globally and help them achieve their career aspirations, Dr Shaikh actively engages with young student entrepreneurs, providing guidance and mentorship as they transition into the real world. Her motivating words to her students are always encouraging: "Cherish your dreams and visions, as they are the blueprints of your ultimate achievements."

In her previous role as the Chief Happiness Officer and Vice President of Student Experience at universities, Dr Shaikh spearheaded various projects and initiatives aimed at promoting happiness and cultivating a positive and joyful environment. One notable accomplishment was the establishment of a Student Happiness Centre, where students could freely share their ideas, suggestions, and aspirations for new projects, extracurricular activities, competitions, and events to enhance their university experience.

Through her remarkable leadership, unwavering dedication, and genuine passion for student success and well-being, Dr Shaikh continues to make a profound impact on the educational landscape, shaping the future of aspiring young minds and fostering a culture of excellence, internationalisation, and happiness within academic institutions.

THE MAKING OF MARIAM

When Dr Shaikh was about 12 years old, the family business was taken over fraudulently by her father's uncle. Multiple court cases ensued as the family tried to retrieve the business, which had been originally set up by her grandfather. The process was expensive, and the family struggled financially, almost overnight going from a privileged and affluent existence, to struggling to make ends meet. The stress took its toll, and Dr Shaikh's mother was hospitalised after suffering a nervous breakdown.

Fearing greatly for her mother's health, this experience took its toll on the young Mariam. She took responsibility for her mother's care, whilst helping her father to accumulate legal papers supporting his case. The judicial battle took over a decade to conclude and affected the whole family. Thankfully, their circumstances began to change when Mariam's father started his own business from scratch. The name of the new company was Cupid, and her father and brother worked from a garage to get it off the ground, while Mariam got the fortuitous chance to learn how to grow a business from the bottom up, a seminal moment in her life and career.

Unfortunately, Mariam's mother passed away, but her father became her "best friend, guide and mentor, who always stressed gender parity, believed that

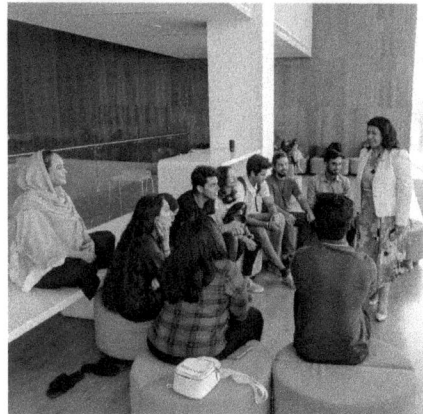

girls should get equal opportunities as boys and was very supportive of [her] future aspirations." As the new business progressed, Mariam was able to continue with her studies and graduated with a BA in Psychology, an MA in Educational Psychology, and, eventually, a PhD in Transformational Educational Leadership.

THE NEXT CHAPTER

Although it was always clear that "from the very beginning, [she] was extremely passionate about cultivating young minds," her pathway into mentorships and empowering students actually started by chance.

When Dr Shaikh's husband was posted to the UAE in the 1980s, she, along with her two children, followed him. As there was only one pre-school to choose from for her 2-year-old daughter, Dr Shaikh decided to open up her home as a school, following the British curriculum. The news soon spread and "before [she] knew it, [she] had close to 10 kids and hired another teacher and classroom assistant." Things escalated from there, and soon The Sunflower Nursery had been formed, with over 80 children in attendance.

However, when Dr Shaikh's husband got a new posting in Dubai, she sold her nursery and followed him. She soon found a position as Principal of a large Indian school, and then became the Manager of the Admissions Office for the University of New Brunswick, based in Canada. Dr Shaikh's desire and ability to mentor and empower her students, helping them in their study choices, encouraging them to be entrepreneurial and pursue their dreams and work hard to achieve became evident when she "sent a hundred students to the University by the second year in Dubai, establishing it as the preferred study destination for students from the UAE and GCC."

She also made a significant contribution in establishing "some of the most reputed foreign university branch campuses in the UAE." Her 35-year contribution to the field was recognised by her name being inscribed on the Al Jalila Foundation wall, a non-profit healthcare organisation founded by Mohamed Bin Rashid Al Maktoum. Her passion for education has not wavered, as she has "now initiated [her] entrepreneurial venture MS Education Consultants, where [she] continues with [her] mission of assisting students globally."

MANAGING MONEY

All successful entrepreneurs know the importance of establishing careful and systematised financial processes, and Dr Shaikh is no exception. "The money we use is not free, neither is it unlimited. Wise use of monetary resources will benefit us in the present and in the future." With this in mind, Dr Shaikh creates a budget plan at the beginning of every month so that she can estimate how much money she will require for events and activities. She tracks any expenses and categorises them as bills, savings or miscellaneous expenditure. Savings go into a bank account and are never used "unless it is an emergency."

Receipts allow her to record the expenditure, so she can evaluate the main areas of expenditure and then calculate how she can spend less in the future. She makes sure to pay her bills before the second week of each month, so that a large part of her outgoings are already out of the way. "This makes it easier to categorise the remaining expenses and the stress of bills is out of the way." Dr Shaikh is keen to point out that working in educational establishments is very different to being an entrepreneur. It's the difference between having a stable monthly and secure income, and invoicing international clients and waiting for them to send payment, which is "most often delayed."

As a self-funding entrepreneur, Dr Shaikh likes to use a budgeting technique which involves dividing money into three parts: 50/30/20 - 50% goes on needs, 30% on

wants and 20% goes to either savings or paying debts.

WOMEN IN DUBAI

"The Dubai you see today is not the Dubai you will see tomorrow." Dr Shaikh always wanted to settle in a different country other than India, so when the opportunity arose she was "ecstatic," especially as Dubai was only a 2.5 hour flight from her home country. It also had the benefit of being a "rapidly developing country offering job opportunities and a tax-free salary."

Many women entrepreneurs will agree with Dr Shaikh, who stipulates that the "UAE encourages women entrepreneurs as it's a safe and secure place to live, and it supports women in business." Dr Shaikh, like many other businesswomen, feels "empowered" by being in Dubai and is convinced that she would not have attained the same level of success in any other part of the world.

She is passionate about promoting all the positive aspects of women working in the UAE, which has the highest number of women listed in Forbes 100 Most Powerful Arab Businesswomen (2020). Dr Shaikh also believes that "the UAE offers more comprehensive support by building an entrepreneurial ecosystem." She highlights the free zones providing licensing packages exclusively for women, such as the Women in Innovation Package, the Women

Entrepreneurship Programme and the Intilaq Programme from the Department of Economic Development.

"Dubai has always taught me the meaning of thinking big!" Dr Shaikh highlights the spectacular architecture scattered all over the city, "the world-class lifestyle," it offers, along with Dubai being a "top 10 global financial centre." It's one of the region's most diversified economies with "over 200 private schools," and expansive amenities, with the added benefit of being able to access two-thirds of the population within eight hours.

Dr Shaikh remarks on how the "UAE is the best place to be now, especially as a woman entrepreneur." She is clearly immersed in the culture, being an active member of a wide range of organisations, including the UAE-Africa Initiative, Advisor of Indian Women in Dubai network, President of the Education Leadership - Commonwealth Entrepreneurs Club and Country Ambassador for the World Women Leadership Congress 2022.

WOMEN AND ENTREPRENEURSHIP

Dr Shaikh suggests that all women must contend with a wide range of challenges in business. "I have certainly faced challenges in my professional career, whether it be the uphill battles of achieving goals or fierce competition. I believe that anyone with smart habits and a positive 'Can Do' attitude can be a success." She suggests that conscious changes to behaviour and attitude could be very rewarding.

She observes that most women feel as though they need to adopt a stereotypically "male" attitude toward business: competitive, aggressive and sometimes harsh. But she believes that, to be a successful female CEO, you must always remain true to yourself and find your own voice, which is key to rising above preconceived expectations.

Turning popular misconception on its head, Dubai is at the global forefront of female empowerment and entrepreneurship in the business sector. According to Dr Shaikh, women hold two-thirds of public sector posts in the UAE and almost a third of senior decision-making positions in the government sector. The changing role of women in Dubai mirrors the Emirates' explosive growth in recent decades.

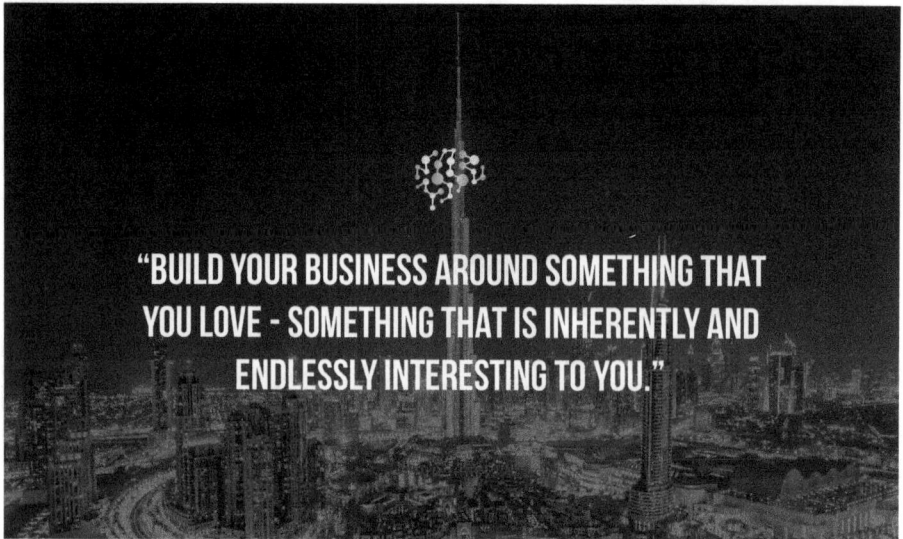

"BUILD YOUR BUSINESS AROUND SOMETHING THAT YOU LOVE - SOMETHING THAT IS INHERENTLY AND ENDLESSLY INTERESTING TO YOU."

ENTREPRENEUR AWARD — DR. MARIAM SALIM SHAIKH HUSEIN

However, "as a female entrepreneur in a male-dominated industry, earning respect becomes a struggle for most women, but living and being a woman entrepreneur in Dubai is a blessing!"

Mariam explains, "the greatest challenge for me was when I first moved from a senior professional role in a university to becoming an entrepreneur." The first thing she had to get used to was not having a secure and regular income, "you have to continuously be on your toes or hustle as it is commonly called, to generate funds."

Not all start-up founders look for investors to help get their businesses off the ground, but those who do, know how difficult the pitching process can be. Dr Shaikh, warns that raising capital is even more difficult for women-owned businesses. "I have not had the need for this yet, but definitely as my business scales up, I will make myself pitch ready."

As a start-up entrepreneur, securing that first contract can be a very challenging endeavour. However, the sense of accomplishment that follows is unparalleled and incredibly rewarding.

When Dr Shaikh had to make the initial difficult pitch when starting her own company, she "held on to the belief that setbacks were not road blocks, but stepping stones on the path to success." Her resilience enabled her to transform her difficult moments into testimonials of strength and determination.

Dr Shaikh is keen to point out that there are times when most women CEOs find themselves in a male-dominated industry or workplace that does not want to acknowledge their leadership role. In response to this, there are some women's groups which provide coworking space for female entrepreneurs. They inspire and encourage female investors to grow and support them through both funding and strategic educational workshops.

"We need to see more women, especially at the top, to change the dynamics, reshape the conversation and to make sure that women's voices are heard and not ignored or overlooked."

MARKETING STRATEGIES

As a seasoned entrepreneur and natural mentor, Dr Shaikh offers some effective marketing strategies to ensure your business gains momentum and can expand:

Effective social media engagement.
Set your brand apart by focusing on excellence.
Operate with a strong purpose and vision.
Use the right tools for search engine optimisation.
Use digital marketing to help reach your target audience.
Word of mouth testimonials from clients add great value.
Network in appropriate groups.
Participate in work-related conferences and workshops.
Discount codes can expedite purchases.
Be aware of consumer demand for environmental commitments.
Get to know your customer.
Customer stories in video, blog, podcast and infographic formats will help boost sales.
Craft your messaging, improve your offer and grow your business and brand.

DUBAI
BUSINESS
LEADERS

TARIQ QUERISHY

CEO OF MAD AND XPONENTIAL GROUP

"Transforming BEFORE you have to is a better option than BECAUSE you have to."

DR JOHN FRANCIS

CEO of ZtartUp.com, Partner at KUBE VC, CEO of Intelligent Beings,
Director of mU Holdings.inc, Fellow of the Royal Society of Arts, Globel
Panel Member of the MIT Technology Review, Gobal Panel Member of
the Harvard Business Review

D r John is known by many names, but he feels the most popular and apt is *#johnofthings*, "because [he is] literally into everything, from music to theatre, dance, fashion, films, sports, religion and politics, you name it, [he has] been there, done that and moved on."

John has indeed moved on and is currently a member of a wide and exhaustive list of organisations, associations, forums & platforms including think tanks such as the World Economic Forum, the World Business Angels Forum, Forbes Business Council and the Economic Corporate Network. As a venture capitalist with Kube VC, he has a long list of start-ups under his belt, investing in commercial products, services, media, and technology sectors. To date, Kube VC has helped support and develop over 120 start-ups, of which five have become unicorn businesses. He is also the CEO of ZtartUp.com, a first of its kind tech business incubator and accelerator based in Dubai with 16 startups onboarded from 9 diverse sectors like health, travel, technology, media, services, trade, tertiary, sports & arts.

"PERCEPTION IS EVERYTHING IN THIS WORLD."

John claims that out of the 365 days of the year, he spends at least 300 of them sitting in the back row of summits and conferences, listening intently and absorbing information because, "it's more about what you do with that knowledge that matters, rather than merely being in the limelight."

Born and brought up in Delhi, India, in a middle-class household of five children. He has travelled extensively, and doesn't show any indication of slowing down. His aliases reflect his persona and identity according to where he lays his hat; *#John1.0* was "India centric" *#John2.0* was UAE centric and *#John3.0* was "GCC/MENA centric." His current stage is being global with *#John4.0* to keep pace with the accelerating Industrial Revolution 4.0 (IR4.0) and he is already into it by touching base with the "Harvards, MITs and Oxfords" of the world.

VERY FOOLISH JOHN

Childhood experiences can be warm and wonderful, but also rough and raw, leaving a lasting mark on a developing psyche. As a schoolboy, on one occasion John entered the classroom a little late and was admonished by his teacher who exclaimed "here comes very foolish John." It may have seemed a flippant remark, but to John it was

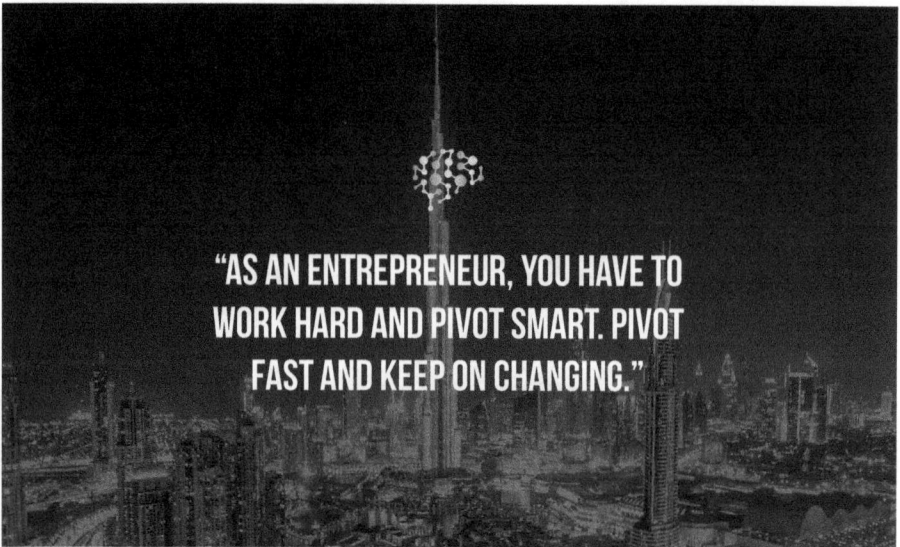

"AS AN ENTREPRENEUR, YOU HAVE TO WORK HARD AND PIVOT SMART. PIVOT FAST AND KEEP ON CHANGING."

damaging, to the extent that he has never really stopped proving to the world that "[he] is not foolish." In fact, John even entitled his debut book **'VFJ - Very Foolish John'**, demonstrating the effect that those three words had on his outlook.

Positively, he took the statement as a source of motivation as opposed to something that crushed his self-confidence. As a realist, he understands that "every man and woman has their shortcomings, but you have to look at the better, positive side." While at school, John was very entrepreneurial, initially earning money as a DJ at school parties, then scaling up and transitioning it into a large and very commercial operation. He not only turned the discs for established grown up parties, he was also invited to work with the British Council, Max Mueller & USIC supporting technicians, set designers and lighting for international cultural events. Still at school, he was working with "top-end theatre groups, performers, artists and musicians," and he found a great passion in particular for the new technology he was being introduced to.

At school, John had a rebellious nature, with hair down to his shoulders, and a refusal to wear a belt or tie. However, what he lacked in formal appearance, he made up for in business acumen. Alongside his schoolboy DJ-ing, John purchased an old-fashioned journalist typewriter and constructed two sets of information to take

ZtartUp.com

CXO DX FUTURE WORKSPACE SUMMIT & AWARDS

ZTARTUP WINS THE
SMART INNNOVATION AWARD 2022

to the Bank Manager. The first outlined his projects and the money he earned from them, and the second outlined his forthcoming projects and his considerable financial projections. Regardless of how successful the 18-year-old John had been with his business endeavours, only if his father agreed to be guarantor would the bank go ahead and loan him the money.

As a technophile in his early twenties, John was networking with big names in sound technology. His big irritation was the short time span that most recording devices had. If a concert was three hours long, he could not record it in its entirety without losing a couple of seconds while he switched the tape around. The dynamic entrepreneur reached out to Akai, Matsushita, Sanyo and the like for information on the latest tech, and he made contact with Sony, who sent a VHS tape recorder on which to record in digital format to try out before it entered the global market, an interaction that changed his whole process. Suddenly, he was able to record top concerts with audiences in their "hundreds and thousands." It gave John "tremendous traction," and he found a new kind of education, not maths or science, but music and theatre. He has now been involved with approximately 300+ theatrical and musical productions in India, encompassing hundreds of cast members at a professional level.

ZTARTUP.COM

Based in Dubai, ZtartUp started in September 2019 just before the COVID pandemic, and during quarantine he saw contractors, team members and staff "just disappear" seemingly overnight. Like many companies, both established and new, John had to decide whether to "continue with brick and mortar, or transfer into a virtual platform." And, as a young company without a developed infrastructure, they decided to continue with the physical office and ZtartUpNetwork was up and running, and the process is simple; they listen to a start-up pitch and if they feel that it fits into the ecosystem, they will "incubate them and take them forward through pitching to investors." There are three elements to their decision-making process, "gut level" meaning they will take a chance on an instinct, "attempt level," they will support a start-up once and see if they have the capability to scale it forward, and "success level," meaning they've found something special, it's a sure-shot thing.

"YOUR CALLING IS NOT PREDESTINED. YOU'LL FIND YOUR CALLING WHEN YOU START MOVING IN THAT DIRECTION, AND RECOGNISE THOSE 'AHA' MOMENTS."

Once on board, budding entrepreneurs are trained, mentored, coached and guided through the process of how to pitch to investors. They are supported with admin, marketing, legal and auditing skills. "We are the only incubator here in Dubai who has got professionals sitting in and around the startups who are in the hub." He makes it clear that it's a community where everyone is on a first name basis, celebrating each other's birthdays and weddings. "Incubation is all about the mentors, coaches, and guides passing on their wisdom, we will only go to them when they need us."

As a Venture Capitalist with Kube VC, John invests in the typical fields of robotics, health, travel and tourism. However, John's personal passion means that they also invest heavily in the arts, films & music. "I think humanity is all about these softer subjects and not about technology. There is no subject which takes you closer to God than any of these creative mediums." John sees it as a mission to be a patron for the arts by helping artists "monetise their creativity."

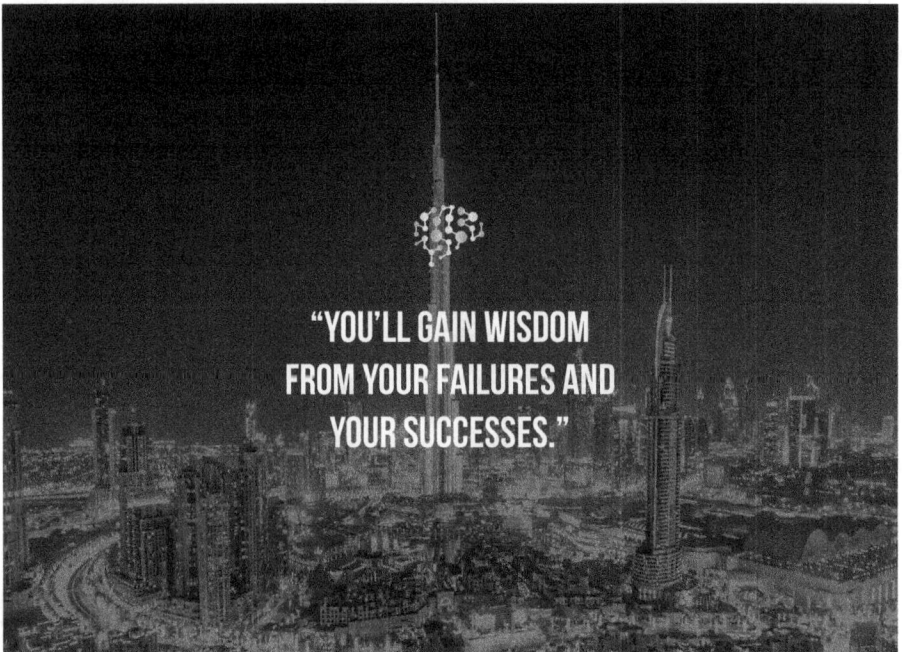

"YOU'LL GAIN WISDOM FROM YOUR FAILURES AND YOUR SUCCESSES."

LEADERSHIP TIPS

"Leadership is inherent in almost everybody, but you should lead by example." For John, if you are unable to do that, then you need to be mentored, coached or advised. He practises what he preaches, and is happy to see his staff learn and transform themselves into entrepreneurs, investing in their early career towards becoming the leaders and CEO's (Chief Enablement Officers) of tomorrow. John also urges "big tech companies" to treat their employees as "individual profit-oriented units, and people who can contribute to the ecosystem."

SPIRITUAL BEINGS

Beyond his fascination with space and technology, John has a strong spiritual side, formed by his love of Christian teachings and also his attraction to Hindu practices and beliefs. Meeting with gurus who had reached "a higher level of existence," and "only interacted with [him] using slips of paper," they told John that people come to them for help with one of three things; health, wealth or career issues. John wanted to understand "these spiritual beings" and was mesmerised by their existence. "They rarely eat yet have tremendous energy." It was at this time he began to realise that there was something more to life that he wanted to search for.

The gurus had told him he was destined for a higher spiritual existence and promised him a position in their ashram, a "blessing" he still keeps in mind today, especially as he has not accumulated material wealth or possessions.

John talks about one particular man he met who had left his home at the age of 14 years, had walked the whole of India on foot and spoke 16 languages fluently. Although a Hindu, this "one religious guy is a doctorate in Christianity," and knows "each page, stanza, word and parable in the Bible." John was shy and humbled in the presence of this spiritual being who had set up a small temple for people to come and gain wisdom from him.

John now practices yoga for "intense meditation to raise [his] life force to a certain level. I have my thousand eyes opening to facilitate all that knowledge that is there in the universe." He particularly enjoys the company of world leaders because he has now reached a level where "mundane, small things don't mean anything."

LOOKING TO THE FUTURE

Like most thought-leaders, John identifies humanity's need for survival as being at the forefront of AI. He suggests that we are already witnessing the decline of the planet with "climate change and temperature rises causing natural calamities that are happening all over the world, like floods, hurricanes, and tornadoes." He also believes that space travel is the inevitable next step if people are to survive.

Looking to the future, John suggests Elon Musk's Neuralink chip could be a game changer. Set up to restore people's vision and mobility by connecting brains to computers. The Neuralink's device could be used for a range of therapeutic uses, to treat conditions like blindness, paralysis, depression. But he has also said that the eventual aim is to create a "general population device" that could connect a user's mind directly to supercomputers and help humans keep up with artificial intelligence. He has also suggested that the device could eventually extract and store thoughts, as "a backup drive for your non-physical being, your digital soul." Although the FDA has given Neuralink approval to conduct its first tests on humans, it's still very early days. However, John's imagination is limitless, and he sees a time when a microchip in the brain could offer you several specialist careers in one lifetime.

DUBAI
BUSINESS
LEADERS

"The deed is worse than the dread, so do
the deed to deaden the dread."

Dee Allen
COO - Global Talent Acquisition Leader

"Failure is about experiences, and if you experience
failure, it makes you come back stronger."

Elias Mbeki
Principal Managing Partner - Real Estate

"Opportunity lies in front of everyone,
so start working, stop thinking, and take
every opportunity offered."

Deeksha Gandotra
Managing Director - Versatile Consultancy

"As a leader, it's crucial to create an environment that fosters autonomy. A bottleneck in the decision-making process only slows things down in business, so empower your teams to make decisions on your behalf by prioritising the customer first. Allow your team to make calculated risks, and even fail at times, because when your team feels empowered and trusted, they will make the right decisions."

Marius Ciavola
CEO, Advisor & Board Member
B2B Marketplaces & Trade Facilitation

BIJAY SHAH

National Director at BNI United Arab Emirates

With a background in banking, insurance, and financial services, Bijay is well positioned to promote networking opportunities through collaboration with local organisations. Under his leadership, the BNI UAE has built a community of people from over 30 nationalities, and diverse age groups, with aims to double its members over the next three years. For Bijay, making connections is a passion, and he particularly enjoys seeing local businesses expand their reach through the BNI network.

Bijay attributes his community values to his upbringing. Originally from Kenya, he spent time in the UK before settling in Dubai, where "serving others" comes in the guise of helping businesses connect. He explains, "that's how I've been brought up and that's what I do... it's all about how we can connect and help others." Having been born in Nairobi to "a very large extended family," his uncles ran the "largest stationary and books distribution company" in East Africa. He remembers spending his childhood "going to the shop and helping, not just in retail but also the distribution wholesale side." From an early age, he was "surrounded by conversations which revolved around business." So, for Bijay, the business was providing a service, and it was that very concept that has stayed with him throughout his career.

"PASSION BY ITSELF
DOESN'T REALLY HELP."

Even as a young child, his extracurricular activities centred on "charity work and helping the less fortunate." Travelling around the world, Bijay observed "people in need," and as one of his uncles was a philanthropist, he was aware of what could be done to serve others, and the impact that it made. His help came in the form of fundraising, facilitating connections, and networking for the financial benefit of others. It's something he mirrors today in his work with BNI UAE.

Bijay attended University in the UK, and, as a person "who wanted to do his own thing," had decided not to follow his father into the family business, but to go into global financial services. He loved the world of banking, it was more than just the money, it was the strategy that excited him. So, he got married in 1998 and moved to the UK in 2001 to work for an American stockbroker firm in London. His role, based in Canary Wharf, required making connections "literally around the neighbourhood."

After about three years, Bijay had "mastered the art of cold calls and sales," before moving to Dubai to work in a financial advisory role. He had been introduced to BNI back in the UK and was keen to join the UAE version, but found that it didn't exist. After some research and a phone call to BNI headquarters in the US, he took up a franchise and developed BNI UAE as a "great way to connect people and help each other." As a keen advocate for personal development, he noticed that the organisation was also capable of impacting people beyond business networking, and he decided to move into the role of director on a full-time basis. His pharmacist wife also came on board, and the couple have been living and working together at BNI UAE for the past 18 years, expanding into other parts of the region like Qatar, Bahrain and Oman.

BNI UAE was extremely successful in generating a culture of mutual support for business people in the area, but for the first six years, there were few profits to be made. Nevertheless, it was more of a passion project for Bijay, and his perseverance paid off, with the organisation eventually becoming "very lucrative." Now, having settled in Dubai, he has "over a thousand members, and many of them are like family." He's proud of his journey, having landed in Dubai without knowing anyone, and almost single-handedly creating an "ecosystem of friends who became friends through the business relationships, and we all count on each other and support each other."

BUSINESS NETWORK INTERNATIONAL

Founded in 1985 by Dr Ivan Meisner, BNI has around 300,000 members across 80 countries and is "probably the largest business network of its kind." With trust and credibility at its heart, an annual fee is paid to join the referral network and become part of a group of people from different industries and in different roles, brought together by shared values and a willingness to commit to each other by referring each other's businesses. Once a week, the BNI holds a breakfast meeting, allowing businesses to gain exposure and build relationships with over 50 companies on a weekly basis.

Building a community of businesses who support and trust each other is mainly achieved through gamification. Through competitions and a scoring system, each business can highlight the sort of things they do. BNI UAE creates numerous events focusing on their core values, which gives businesses the recognition that they strive for. Bijay openly embraces gamification, and continues to focus on building a culture of life-long learning and growth in the organisation.

The early morning breakfast meetings start at 6am, and those who attend once a week are early risers, eager to build and connect before a busy day's work. For Bijay,

who has a full social and business life himself, with networking engagements and collaborative meetings with other associations, it was important to train his own body clock to wake up early and properly utilise all hours of the day.

A VISIONARY LEADER

Bijay suggests that most people are mistaken in thinking that "the streets [of Dubai] are paved with gold." However, the city's culture of technological innovation has made it a "recognised centre when it comes to business development, networking and geographical location." He praises how easy it is for "anybody to come here and set up a business," particularly as a hub for networking, attracting a "melting pot" of people from around the globe, all keen to build connections.

Although Dubai is most commonly known for its bustling tourism industry, Bijay has also recognised a growing number of start-ups gravitating towards the city to source funding, something he attributes to the advanced technology attracting VCs and start-ups interested in tech-based innovation. Interestingly, he also suggests that Dubai is soon to become a "significant player" in space technology due to the visionary leadership's interest in that area. For Bijay, it's clear that Dubai, with its ambitious, forward-thinking goals, is quickly transforming into one of the world's most attractive cities to work and live in.

A BUSINESS LEADER

Bijay considers a business leader to be someone who makes a significant impact on people's lives. It's more than creating an organisation and impacting stakeholders such as employees, customers, shareholders and vendors; it's about reaching people indirectly through your social media profiles, books, articles and public speaking events. For Bijay, a successful business leader commands respect for their skills and knowledge.

He makes sure to develop his own leadership persona by studying self-development and business books, as well as observing his uncle, who ran the family business back in Kenya, as a prime example of a successful businessman. Whenever he wasn't sure how to act or respond to certain situations, his first port of call was to ask himself what his uncle would do, as a role model. According to Bijay, mentorship doesn't necessarily have to come from someone at a higher level, it can also be from someone in the opposite position. For example, he considers his 16-year-old son as a mentor, whose experiences growing up have provided his father with food for thought on many occasions.

"THEODORE ROOSEVELT ONCE SAID, 'PEOPLE DON'T CARE HOW MUCH YOU KNOW, UNTIL THEY KNOW HOW MUCH YOU CARE'."

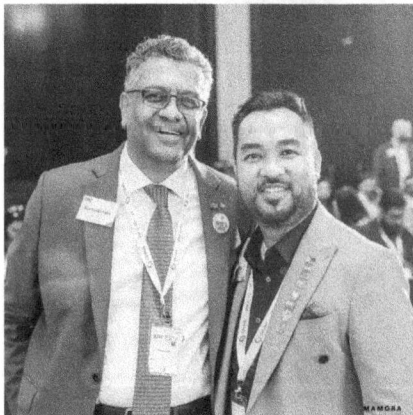

Apart from putting in "time and hard work," nurturing trust and credibility in long-term relationships is another skill Bijay associates with being a strong business leader. Whilst having the ability to "stand up and articulate what you want" is a skill that can be learned, he suggests that the most important attribute, and one that you're perhaps just born with, is integrity. He references Warren Buffett, "when you shake his hand you know, and if you can have values like that, it will take you a long way."

COMMUNICATION

A typical day for Bijay is to firstly check his emails, then WhatsApp and LinkedIn, phone calls, and meeting people face to face or virtually. He suggests that all this communication "actually cuts on your productivity" because technology "brings in so much clutter, it's difficult to keep yourself organised." Interestingly, he refers back to the hybrid model brought in during COVID and observes a generational attitude towards going into the office to "physically interact with people." Bijay suggests that the younger workforce choosing to work from home will lose out on developing core communication skills.

HUDDLES

Bijay is often on the road with "a balance of social and community engagement and strategising." He insists there is "no such thing as work-life balance," and sometimes work requires 100% of your time and effort. "It's not about having balance, it's about having harmony." Time blocking and calendarising are two strategies which Bijay relies on heavily to manage his time. He also suggests delegation and collaboration as being vital "skills" which need to be developed, "because it's all about team and having the right people in the right place." Bijay has daily "huddles" where he checks in with his team for a catch-up, which works well in establishing roles and responsibilities within the team.

CHANGING THE WORLD

To change the world for the better, Bijay promotes the concept of a "circular economy." Conservation and biodiversity are essential in changing the trajectory of the planet, and it's all about "reusing, recycling and repurposing materials." Sustainable agriculture is another concept close to Bijay's heart, and he has noticed that, even in the shiny high-tech city of Dubai, with all their space exploration endeavours and embracing the new technological innovations, they are looking back to what life was like a hundred years ago and working on offering residents a plot of land where they can grow their own food.

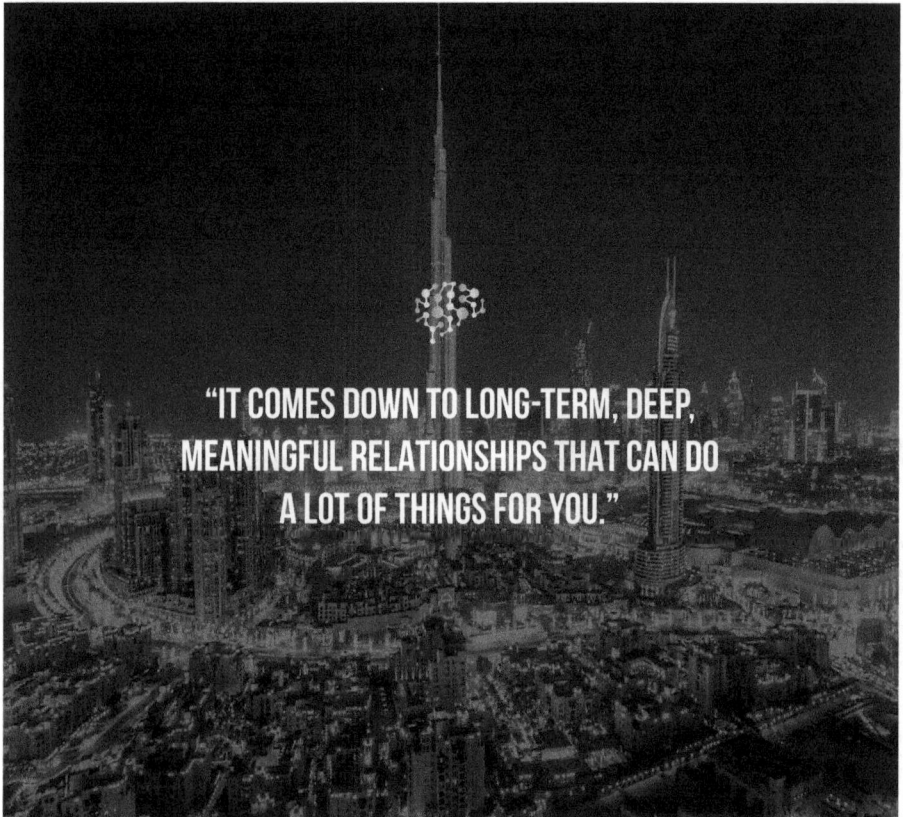

"IT COMES DOWN TO LONG-TERM, DEEP, MEANINGFUL RELATIONSHIPS THAT CAN DO A LOT OF THINGS FOR YOU."

DUBAI
BUSINESS
LEADERS

ELENI KITRA

CEO of KITRA Inclusive Leadership Partners, Top 100 Asia's Women Power Leaders 2023, CIO Times Influential Women to watch 2023, Business & Tech Executive, Board, DEI Advisor, Global speaker, Author

B orn in Athens to Greek parents, and married to a "Greek Australian she met at University," Eleni has been able to embed her culture and heritage into the life she has now led in Dubai for the past twelve years. Overall, three key words have really defined her life journey, both personally and professionally, purpose, change and force.

AN ENTREPRENEUR AT HEART

Eleni has built, grown, and revolutionised with measurable impact on a number of global businesses in diverse industries. In all her years in the corporate world she feels blessed to have worked for some of the most "amazing" companies, meet inspiring people, and travel around the world. She launched Playstation and became market leader, commercialised Multichoice Pay TV, co-built the Digital media industry and drove Omnicom to market lead for twelve consecutive years. When she moved to Dubai, she established META (ex Facebook) as the leading platform across the mobility and automotive Industry in the Middle East. She is an active member of the MENA Business community and today she serves as Advisor to several tech-based startups, and co-chairs the Transformational Business Leaders Committee at Capital Club Dubai.

PASSIONATE MENTOR AND PEOPLE EQUALITY AMBASSADOR

As a global leader in supporting women in Tech, she has spearheaded women in leadership across the world, and has served on the global DEI board in Facebook. She launched the #startyourengines initiative in KSA, founded the Women in Mobility GCC Forum and several other communities. She is also a member of the global initiative 10M Moms and a founding member of the UAE Chapter of UN Women Unstereotype Gender. She is the Founder and CEO of KITRA Inclusive Leadership Partners, a modern DEI company, with the mission to make the workplace a better place for all and help companies to build diverse and inclusive organisations and achieve organisational excellence.

COMMITTED TO YOUTH

As a mother of two GenZ, she is fully faced with recognizing the immense value of this generation as the future of our country and society's main agents of change and progress. She has committed to contributing to youth education and mentoring young entrepreneurs in collaboration with VCs and Educational institutions. Eleni is chairing the Middlesex Innovation and Entrepreneurship Hub and she is a senior lecturer in Leadership, Innovation and Digital marketing.

BUSINESS TRANSFORMATION IN THE MIDDLE EAST ACROSS

In recent years, the Middle East has witnessed a profound transformation across various industries. Eleni, a prominent figure in the business landscape, highlights a significant paradigm shift, particularly in the automotive sector, where advanced technology has given rise to what is now referred to as the "mobility industry." This evolution extends beyond individual car ownership and sporadic taxi usage, encompassing a wide array of transportation methods such as e-bikes, e-scooter rentals, ride-sharing, and ride-hailing applications. This expansion has effectively redefined mobility as a service, resulting in notable changes in consumer behaviour.

In response to this dynamic shift, Eleni spearheaded the implementation of innovative strategies, services, collaborative initiatives, and novel advertising approaches. Her initial focus was on the Middle East and North Africa (MENA) region, subsequently expanding these initiatives on a global scale. Eleni's strategic vision aligned seamlessly with the region's commitment to achieving net-zero emissions, the emergence of compact transportation models, and the societal repercussions of the COVID-19 pandemic. This convergence enabled her to forecast the likely trajectory of the mobility industry over the next five to ten years.

After nearly a decade with Meta, Eleni embarked on her own entrepreneurial journey, armed with a wealth of experience and insights into the transformative forces shaping the business landscape in the Middle East and beyond. Since then, she's focused on creating and guiding purposeful businesses that combine people, innovation, and growth.

DIVERSITY AND INCLUSION

With nearly three decades of experience in the technology sector, Eleni possesses a unique vantage point for assessing not only the industry's transformations but also global developments. She holds a deep passion for Diversity and Inclusion (D&I), a concept she's delighted to see gaining prominence within the tech sector. Eleni notes that D&I has evolved into a strategic imperative, evident in organisations publicly outlining their end goals and strategies in this regard. Additionally, entities are now subject to assessments based on their diversity and inclusion index, a positive development benefiting the entire industry.

As a female business leader, Eleni underscores that gender equality in the workplace transcends mere equity; it extends to the substantial economic contributions made by women, estimated by Eleni to range from 6 to 13 trillion dollars in global GDP by 2025. The empowerment of women, across social, educational, economic, and political dimensions, has advanced significantly. Eleni emphasises a new facet: there is a growing demand for empowering women to regain their well-deserved positions in both society and the business world.

EMPOWERING WOMEN IN DUBAI

When contemplating the future of the technology sector, Eleni envisions a higher presence of women leaders, particularly in entrepreneurial domains. She highlights a significant trend, stating, "efforts to assist women in establishing their own companies are substantial, with a remarkable 80% increase in the number of female entrepreneurs in the UAE recently."

Dubai offers a plethora of programs and incentives tailored for businesswomen, facilitating swift company establishment. Eleni's experience illustrates this efficiency, as she was able to establish her own enterprise within a mere week, with all the necessary documentation and financial accounts seamlessly organised.

Eleni collaborates with businesses dedicated to advancing female empowerment across diverse industries. Notably, she underscores the distinguishing factor between the UAE and other nations in terms of women in business. Once the government embraced this initiative, it catalysed a widespread shift, and there was no turning back. This progressive leadership in Dubai is reflected in her experiences, as she sometimes finds herself facing more challenges in the European entrepreneurial landscape than in Dubai.

THE POWER OF THE PLATFORM

In 2017, a historic milestone was achieved as women were granted the right to drive in Saudi Arabia, a country frequently visited by Eleni during her tenure at Meta. Responding to this newfound freedom, Eleni launched the "Start Your Engines" program, a concerted effort to connect female consumers with automotive brands, providing women with invaluable information about cars. This initiative was presented at an event attended by more than one thousand women, equipping them with the knowledge they needed. Witnessing the acceptance of women drivers in Saudi Arabia, Eleni celebrated the sight of the first female driver with a sense of relief, gratitude, and profound happiness. It signified the normalisation of something that women in developed nations often take for granted, all made possible through the platform's influence.

But, for any plan to work well, it needs a strong foundation. Eleni faced a number of obstacles when working with a financial institution to help women in sub-Saharan countries access financial services. Problems like gender discrimination, lack of financial education, legal barriers, and even cultural norms, resulted in slow progress.

"DON'T START FROM THE CHALLENGES, START FROM THE OPPORTUNITIES."

GEN Z

With two children in their early twenties, Eleni has firsthand insight into the daily lives of Generation Z. She's struck by their "distinctive thinking, rapid pace, tech-savviness, and their preference for efficient problem-solving using their intellect rather than just investing hours." Recently, when leading a discussion event for Gen Z, Eleni was pleasantly surprised by how many of them consider their parents as role models and are eager to express their gratitude for what the previous generation has provided. Eleni sees this as a significant opportunity for companies to harness the energy, knowledge, and potential of Gen Z. While they may lack experience, they bring a fresh perspective and innovative ways of approaching challenges.

KITRA INCLUSIVE LEADERSHIP PARTNERS

Eleni's steadfast belief in the importance of treating individuals in the workplace with utmost respect became evident during her tenure on the Diversity and Inclusion Board at Meta. This experience served as the catalyst for her decision to establish her own company, dedicated to empowering individuals to excel in their professional environments, thereby enhancing both economic and social outcomes for businesses.

In her role as CEO of KITRA Inclusive Leadership Partners, Eleni is committed to guiding organisational leaders in fostering inclusivity and cultivating a culture of trust that fosters a sense of belonging among employees. Eleni firmly believes that when inclusive leadership is established, it paves the way for smooth operations and improved financial results. KITRA Inclusive Leadership Partners collaborates with a diverse clientele, including global brands, family-owned enterprises, and startups. The support provided primarily revolves around the development of strategic frameworks, mitigating unconscious biases, integrating inclusive language, and assisting individuals in realising their personal objectives within the workplace.

WORK AND PLAY IN DUBAI

Dubai's dynamic and rapidly evolving landscape infuses Eleni with a sense of youthful energy and vitality. What was once a humble fishing village has blossomed into a thriving metropolis of over three million residents hailing from across the globe, establishing itself as a global networking hub of unparalleled significance. Eleni herself has had the privilege of connecting with thousands of individuals, an opportunity she believes she might not have encountered had she remained in her native Greece.

With aspirations to expand her business across the region and support the Start Up Ecosystem, Eleni recently assumed the role of Chair at the innovation hub within Dubai's Middlesex University. This position enables her to synergise academia, corporate entities, and government stakeholders, contributing to the advancement of Dubai's vibrant entrepreneurial ecosystem.

At the heart of Dubai's ambitions lies the Dubai Economic Agenda (D33), a strategic initiative aimed at doubling the city's economic size within the coming decade and cementing its position among the world's top three global cities. D33 encompasses an impressive portfolio of 100 transformative projects designed to propel Dubai into a new era of economic prosperity and global prominence.

"THERE IS ALWAYS DANGER WHERE THERE IS POWER."

ADAM RIDGWAY

FOUNDER AND CEO OF ONE MOTO - LAST MILE ELECTRIC VEHICLES

"If we break down a typical life span, the first 20 years are focused on education, the next 10, is finding out your career path. The last 20 or so years are about reaping the rewards, so the 30 years we have left, isn't very much to make a difference.

Don't get bogged down with the idiosyncrasies of life, or take yourself too seriously. Find your purpose, that one thing you love, give it everything you've got for as long as you can. This creates a successful, rewarding life."

ALEX MEURER

Entrepreneur, Investor, YouTuber

W orking as an engineer for a machine construction company was never going to be enough for Alex Meurer. He was focused on somehow someday working for himself, earning his own money, and being his own boss. However, when he accidentally came across the term bitcoin in 2010 while surfing the internet, he couldn't have imagined how quickly and dramatically this new kind of money would change his life.

He decided to leave his 9-5 job and trade full time when he began to make more money during a 30 minute lunch break than he did working all day, and he's never looked back since. Known as AM Crypto, Alex has been left penniless seven times and homeless on several occasions, but he now lives in one of the most expensive residential buildings in Dubai.

As a cryptotrader, Alex analyzes patterns, algorithms, and statistical models. So it's not surprising that he claims there is a mathematical formula for luck that includes a series of events that line up. Regardless of fate or destiny, Alex admits that it's the people you meet along the way that can help you achieve success. From his friend in Germany, who introduced him to a profitable way to invest in bitcoin, to the multiple and highly lucrative jet fuel deals that 'fell into [his] lap'. He also believes in the power of affirmation and has a vision board, which he can see from all parts of his apartment.

"FAILURE IS INEVITABLE, BUT YOU JUST NEED TO PICK YOURSELF UP AND LEARN FROM IT."

A montage of images that helps him visualise his dreams; owning a Bugatti and a private jet, becoming a billionaire, earning more crypto, having 100,000 YouTube subscribers, and visiting Tokyo. On his way to seeing his vision board materialise, he is happy to share his knowledge and experience with budding crypto investors through his various social media platforms.

He lives by the maxim that "it doesn't matter how many times you fail, as long as you believe you can still make it." Citing Musk, Bezos, and Gates as his heroes, today Alex has multiple businesses and believes integrity, consistency, honesty, and transparency are what make a great leader.

THE DELIGHT OF DUBAI

When he first came to Dubai in August 2018, Alex felt it was too hot! Having spent 7 years in Paris and 4 years in Kyiv, the extreme heat was a shock to the system, and he was relieved to get back home. However, a couple of years later, during a stopover on his way back from the Maldives, Dubai managed to change Alex's mind. Staying at the Skyview Hotel and visiting the Dubai Mall left a good impression, and after returning a couple of times for various projects, he eventually settled in Dubai. He now has multiple companies, including a hedge fund, a car rental platform, and a club in Greece.

Dubai has many delights, but it's also expensive, so Alex wouldn't advise anyone to move to the city "unless they are making at least $200,000 per year. For networking, it's great, but you have to be based here, show commitment to the place, and earn people's trust." He advises that although you may get introduced to lots of different people, you have to be persistent and instill confidence. "If you come here with the idea that you're going to make easy money, you're going to be disappointed."

After a few years of networking and some good investments, everybody knows him in the crypto space in Dubai, and he often gets recognised, probably due to his social media presence.

For now, Alex is happy and thinks Dubai, in the future, will expand on its reputation as the number one crypto and blockchain hub in the world. Also, he believes real estate will continue to grow as a sector, as will the service industry.

EDUCATION AND MINDSET

"I would put my own success down to having a positive mindset, and I believe it's an extremely important part of reaching one's full potential." Alex believes what we should be doing in schools is teaching students how to develop the right mindset. Whether they want to be in a 9-5 job or own their own business, the right mindset could be the difference between success and failure. Also, instead of forcing them to learn specific subjects, students should be given the opportunity to study things they have a real interest in. "If we made subjects optional rather than mandatory, I think students would be more successful in school. Obviously, there needs to be a framework, such as basic math, a second language, etc., but other subjects like philosophy should not be mandatory."

Reflecting on his childhood, it never occurred to him that he could not do anything he wanted to. "If I told my parents I wanted to be a fireman, astronaut, or lawyer, they would encourage me. But that all changes when you get to school. Suddenly that positive mindset goes, and you get negative influences from outside." In Germany, he suggests that negativity continues throughout life. "If I had an idea, they would think I was crazy or stupid and that my idea wouldn't work." But when he

moved away and started living in other countries, he found that people "were more open to ideas and trying new things - what would be the worst thing that could happen?"

To counteract the negative mindset he has experienced throughout his life, Alex has intentions to do some philanthropic work building schools in developing countries, "which could develop a positive mindset."

FROM FAILURE TO SUCCESS

Alex moved from Germany to Paris mainly because of the regulations concerning cryptocurrency, and his plan was to make $1m within 5 years. However, after a series of setbacks and a lack of investors, his funds diminished, and he was left with only 5000 euros. He made the decision to move away from Paris, "which was pretty expensive," and base himself in Kyiv, "where the cost of living was much cheaper." He moved there, went back to the drawing board, and started again. This time, he made sure he learned how to read charts and patterns for cryptocurrency by watching YouTube channels and using Google. This information proved invaluable, as he began making a profit within a few weeks. "My initial goal for the end of the year was to turn my 5000 euros into 25,000 euros. I'm happy to say I made that within the first month of trading, and by the end of the year I had made almost 200,000 euros." After suffering many setbacks and failures, his mindset and perseverance won, and he succeeded in turning 5000 euros into over 2 million euros within 10 months of trading.

DEFINING SUCCESS

For Alex, the secret of success is how you determine it. He suggests that everyone has different goals, and "as long as you accomplish all the goals that you set out to create," then that is success. It's obvious that Alex's success is wrapped up in the money he makes. He enjoys what money can buy, the fast cars, private planes, and yachts. But on a more simple level, and having tasted, even for just a moment, what poverty feels like, success for Alex is "if I don't have to look at my bank account for the rest of my life anymore, do whatever I want, and have the freedom to travel when and wherever I want."

UNDER PRESSURE

When Alex was younger, he hadn't yet developed the tools needed to deal with stress. He remembers a time when he had very little money, and it caused stress. Perhaps this is his motivation, never to be poor again. Now in his 40s, his elixir to youth is to simply "walk away from it, mentally and physically, don't fight it, it doesn't matter how much money is involved, if it starts to look too complicated or looks as if it will cause too much stress, I just don't do it."

Of course, Alex is now in a position where he can afford to walk away from stress and pressure. He can look back to remind himself of what he has already accomplished, and look forward to where he wants to go. It's a great motivator and an effective way to deal with pressure.

THE DIGITAL ANSWER TO CURRENCY AND COLLECTABLES

Alex gives out a lot of advice on his social media channels, and he thinks the next big thing we're going to see in the near future will be blockchain, NFTs (non-fungible tokens), and increased hash power for PCs.

There are so many potential use cases for blockchain, but one of the most obvious applications focuses on a way that people can get paid instantly instead of waiting for a wire to come through, which can take 3-5 days. If a logistics company delivering goods from A-B can get paid instantly, they can then transport more goods quickly instead of waiting for the payment to go through.

Also, NFTs have so many potential use cases. An NFT is really a 'one-of-a-kind' asset in the digital world, so it can't be interchanged. For example, if you want to buy the Mona Lisa but don't have enough money, you may approach a group of friends or investors, and they will all take a share of it. So the Mona Lisa becomes fractionalised as an NFT. In the same way crypto-currency works, NFTs are recorded on a shared ledger, which is basically the blockchain.

Hash power, or hash rate, is fundamentally the power that a computer uses to run different hashing algorithms. These algorithms allow cryptocurrency transactions. There are always new machines coming out that are more energy efficient, and this would make miners more profitable. In the future, we will probably be using quantum computers, which may prove more effective.

REST AND RELAXATION

"Physical and mental wellbeing are definitely important to me. I ensure I always eat healthily at least five days a week. I also exercise, and I think that's really good for my mental health because it leaves me in a relaxed state afterwards. It allows me to get a complete break from all the stress and gives me a change of scenery. They say a change is as good as a rest, and so each month I leave Dubai and go somewhere else, either a different location or a different country, it just recharges me.

VISION BOARDS

The benefits of vision boards are anecdotal, with little scientific research confirming their effectiveness. However, many very successful people swear by the power of displaying images and text to manifest hopes, dreams, and goals. Alex's vision board acts as a continual motivation, but for others, vision boards can be a way of embedding aspirations into their subconscious. Whatever the reason, it is indisputable that vision boards help with self-awareness and reflection, which in turn can invoke success and help goals become reality.

Vision boards don't necessarily need to be physical, you could have one as your screensaver or on your phone. There are even apps available that include inspirational music. What matters most is that it is in a place where you can view it frequently throughout the day.

In order to make your own vision board, you first need to understand what it is that you want to achieve and identify the specifics. Alex's board focuses mainly on tangible items, but boards could be about developing better relationships, finding love, improving health, financial goals, travel, career, or, in fact, anything that reflects your aspiration for a positive life.

CREATE YOUR OWN VISION BOARD

Creating your own vision board can be a simple, fun, and reflective activity. Alex recommends following this simple process, then step back and visualise your goals and intentions.

Format (choose a platform - poster, screensaver, phone background, Pinterest board etc)
Goals   (be specific and focused on what you want to achieve. Don't get too detailed)
Visuals (select relevant imagery, quotes, text which affirm your aspirations)
Layout (spend time creating a visually pleasing layout which is clear and concise)
Personalise (include a photo of yourself and maybe some of your own doodles or artwork)
Display (exhibit it where you can see it regularly throughout the day)
Review (once a year review and change imagery to reflect your goals and aspirations)

"YOU WILL NEVER ACHIEVE YOUR GOAL IF YOU'RE NOT WILLING TO TAKE A CERTAIN AMOUNT OF RISK."

DUBAI
BUSINESS
LEADERS

"When you come across a big problem, don't panic, just break down the big problem into small problems and the solution will become simple and easier to solve."

Rahul Duragkar
Founder and Managing Director - EmitechGroup

"Through it all, it was hard work, integrity and love for the city and the work that I did that propelled me forward."

Shahram Safai
Partner - Afridi & Angell Legal Consultants

"If work offers you a sense of purpose, it will be a big contributor to your overall happiness!"

Sheeba Hasnain
Senior PMO & Digital Transformation Specialist

"Find your purpose because it's very important for you to know why you are doing what you are doing. Your purpose drives your passion, but you have to be persistent in your journey because, as an entrepreneur, you will get knocked back multiple times. But be patient because the joy is in the journey, not the destination."

Siddiq Farid
Founder & CEO - Smart Crowd

KATLEEN PENEL

Entrepreneur, Keynote Speaker, Lecturer,
Mentor, HR & Hospitality Specialist

F or Katleen, having grown up in her parent's hotel in Belgium means that the spirit of hospitality runs through her DNA. Educated in the hotel industry from childhood, taught in prestigious hotel schools and working as a consultant for a number of hotels has led her to the belief that "the hospitality industry is the fine print of our society." Nevertheless, whilst she feels "privileged to have grown up in it, as it made her who she is," She explains that there's one big downfall, in that you "always have to smile."

The hospitality industry is something that many take for granted, yet when done properly and with a certain level of professionalism, it becomes an art. It is also one of the most important industries, an essential and influential part of an economy and one of the biggest employers in the world, encompassing a wide range of skills. There is nothing nicer than sitting down to a well cooked meal in a clean, comfortable and welcoming environment, where the chef has true passion and expertise, or sinking into a snug bed with crisp white sheets in a pristinely presented room, yet the people who make this happen are mostly invisible.

"CONNECT, CONNECT, CONNECT. YOUR NETWORK IS YOUR NET WORTH"

Katleen suggests that "when you grow up in hospitality, you develop a military discipline." Putting people and customer excellence at the centre requires a dedication to achieving both your own exceptionally high standards, and a strong hierarchy where everyone knows their role and their individual responsibilities.

IT'S IN THE BLOOD

Coming from a family of entrepreneurs, Katleen realises that she's been born into a family with some wealth. Growing up, she remembers never feeling part of her social environment in school, during the 1970s and 1980s. She recalls having nice possessions and always being well-dressed, taking holidays abroad, and her mother having weekly shopping sprees where she would spoil her two daughters with the latest fashions, amounting to the modern-day equivalent of 2000 Euros.

Nevertheless, this wealth came at a price. The hospitality industry never rests and when her mother gave birth to Katleen, she left her for a month in the hospital to be looked after by the nurses, so her mother could get back to the business. Katleen was always perplexed when people called her "a fighter" as she felt she had nothing to fight for, coming from "a good background" and having been "treated well by her parents, she had everything as a child." However, she puts her strong survival instinct down to having been left by her mother in her first month of life. "I became a survivor... everything was for the business, everything was for the hospitality, and I have always grown up like that."

Katleen's family history speaks to a generational passion for the service industry. Her grandmother was a cook, and her grandfather was an architect. And after the second world war, they decided to combine their skills and open a hotel. Using his meticulous attention to detail, her grandfather trained the housekeeping staff, while her grandmother ran the restaurant. She talks about her earliest memories of being in the hotel, "as a child of three or four years of age, sitting behind the bar of my grandmother's café rinsing the glasses in the afternoon when it was still quiet." She still pictures the café now, with all its little details and the ambience of guests chatting and drinking coffee.

Growing up meeting so many different people, from different walks of life enabled Katleen to develop strong social skills, and she's someone who instantly comes across as open, warm and approachable. Watching her grandmother chat to strangers, she understood, even as a little girl, that the role was much more than just serving drinks. There is nothing stuffy about Katleen, as her familiarity is tamed with a strong sense of professionalism. She can put anyone at ease without encroaching on their space, and that delicate balance takes a lot of skill.

THE TRADE

Katleen's parents later bought their own hotel, 'Hotel Penel' previously known as the 'Hotel la Renommée'. Observing her parents' successful business management, she set her sights on becoming a manager herself, and decided to attend college. However, failing her German language exam meant that she didn't get to graduate, so she had to pivot and attend a well-regarded Hotel School Spermalie. Despite everything, she remained determined, eventually achieving the position of becoming the first female Maître d'hotel in Belgium and proving that hospitality was in her blood. Even now, Katleen states, "I always go for the big achievement, when I do something, I want to be the best."

Having graduated from the hotel school, she received a job offer to manage the Food and Beverage department in a hotel in Brussels, but was stopped by her parents, who wanted her to work at the family hotel. So, Katleen started working at Hotel Penel, and then took leave to travel and "gain some

knowledge." In 2008, she arrived at the Kempinski Hotel in Bruges, the first five-star hotel in Belgium. There, she spent a year as the HR and Training coordinator and PA to the General Manager before moving on to a larger role, straying from hospitality to work for an investment company as the Director of Human Resources.

Working alongside the CEO Michel Verhaeren, they took over more than fifteen companies and created a new HR department & company synergies. Her skills were easily transferable, as in the hotel business, they would have a wide range of staff with different HR requirements. In fact, she implemented some of the hospitality industry processes to "create a customer service orientated building industry."

THE CALLING OF DUBAI

Katleen is continually chasing her ambition, and Dubai has allowed her to dream big and grow faster. The lack of investment in Europe was holding her back, as she explains, "in Europe it's very difficult to get a loan to work in hospitality or to start your own restaurant." She describes the typical formula for European restaurants as having a focus on classic French cuisine in pursuit of a Michelin star. There are a number of chefs involved in the ecosystem and there is a professionalisation of the industry in so far as "they have their own concepts, different businesses and academies." Whereas Dubai has the money to invest but lacks, on many occasions, the high level of service that Katleen is used to and has grown to expect.

In general, she suggests that the absence of high-quality service stems from a lack of discipline, not just in the hospitality business but in the world in general. We want to do things politically correct, but people need leadership and clear guidance.

She sees this global lack of discipline as stemming from our government leaders, and uses the handling of COVID as an example of the difference in leadership between Dubai and Europe. During lockdown there were major lay-offs, and Katleen maintains that since there is no social safety net provided in Dubai, people had contingency plans already in place, whereas, in Europe, people had a very different attitude because they received money to stay at home. According to Katleen, Europe, had no clear future perspectives during Covid time, where Dubai was clear and announced, once they were open again, they would never close, but, instead, safely monitor the situation, and make sure that everybody could keep on working in safe environments. As she explains, "the vibe and entrepreneurial behaviour is set by the leadership of the ruler."

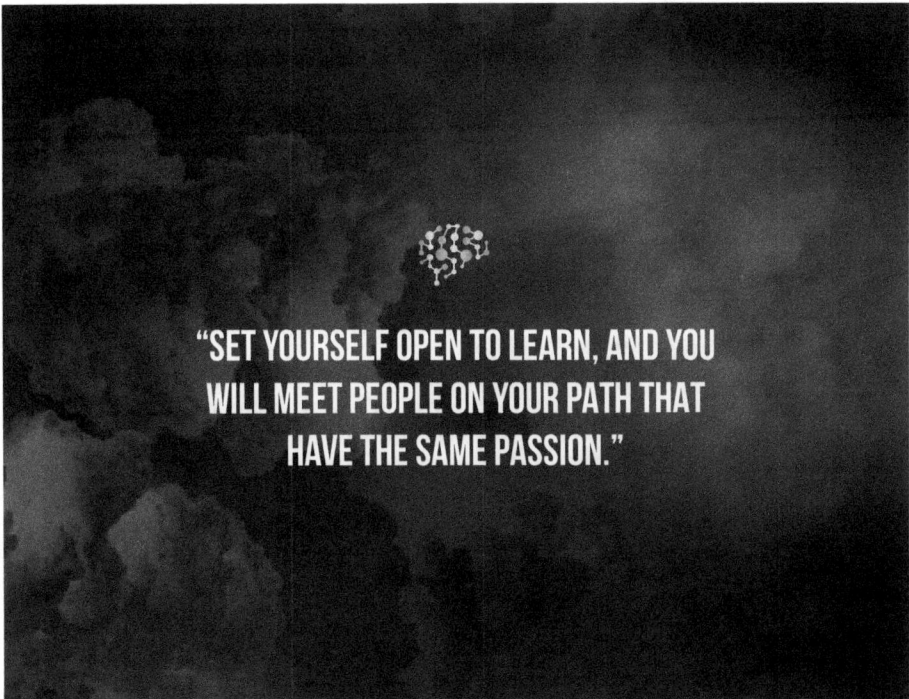

"SET YOURSELF OPEN TO LEARN, AND YOU WILL MEET PEOPLE ON YOUR PATH THAT HAVE THE SAME PASSION."

In 2019, she took on a role as an Ambassador to bring Belgian clients to EXPO 2020, which was then postponed due to the lockdown. However, the super efficient and organised Katleen had already done a lot of the groundwork in preparation, "I made sure that my Belgium clientele knew I was in Dubai, and I did events on demand which tested things, but also allowed me to get to know the right people."

Since moving to Dubai, she has embraced the new cultural landscape, and has adopted Dubai's vision for the future. She admires their entrepreneurial spirit but suggests that it needs to be accompanied by "people who want to go the extra mile and have training." For Katleen, she is in the right place at the right time, "because they have the vision." Enthusiastically, she claims that she is the right person to guide the expansion of more hotels in the region, "it's such a cosmopolitan city and so central, I can fly to more places from Dubai than I can from Brussels."

Katleen is never far away from her great passion and feels the need to support and inspire people in the industry. She confesses to being "always critical," but that is down to her expertise and professionalism in high-end hospitality. She expects good service but also good behaviour from the clientele and will be quick off the mark if she observes staff being mistreated. Teaching is something that has always come naturally to her, having spent 18 years as a teacher in the practical experience of hotel work. However, with a Master's degree in Economics, it's not just the practical side of hotels that she focuses on; payroll services, business systems, automation, and mergers and acquisitions are all areas in Katleen's remit.

THE GLORY OF EXCELLENCE

As founder of 'The Glory of Excellence', a global network for high-end hospitality, Katleen has found an outlet for her passion, focused on delivering the highest quality experience in hotel, food and beverage. She also has an opportunity to work with the other love of her life, her daughter Petra. Initially based in Amsterdam, they have recently expanded to Dubai and together, support professionals in hospitality to grow from one, to two, to three Michelin stars. They also showcase real talent by providing training, coaching to chefs and also offering consulting and hospitality services. They also run an agency for those chefs who have reached the pinnacle of their careers and want to share their knowledge, through performances at road shows, workshops and master classes.

The dynamic duo also create exclusive culinary business networks for those with an appreciation for high-end gastronomy. These events include a fine dining experience for eighteen entrepreneurs, who receive the opportunity to savour the gastronomic delights of top chefs, listen to an inspirational speech from a keynote speaker, and importantly, use the opportunity to connect with fellow entrepreneurs.

Katleen is all about connecting, sharing knowledge and learning constantly to improve her practice. 'The Glory of Excellence' podcast is just another way she achieves her aim of sharing hospitality expertise, with guests ranging from chefs and entrepreneurs to experts in the service industry. Conversations encourage sharing knowledge and insights as well as brainstorming ideas, really bringing the industry into a new space, where excellence in service is paramount, and a huge part of a sophisticated, civilised and very privileged lifestyle.

"IF YOUR DREAM DOESN'T SCARE YOU, IT MEANS THAT IT'S NOT BIG ENOUGH."

DUBAI
BUSINESS
LEADERS

SAM SINGH

FOUNDER & CHIEF EXEC
OF PROPERTECHNOLOGIES LTD
LEAD CONVERSION PLATFORM

THREE NUGGETS FOR BUSINESS

THE 'BE TO HAVE' SPIRAL

All change and aspiration starts from within. To have something, you have to be willing to do something. To do something, you have to be willing to become someone. Becoming someone means you have to be willing to change from within.

SHORT-TERM PLANNING FOR LONG-TERM GAIN

The rate of change in the world is now at rocket speed, and therefore long-term planning is futile. Be agile and use a series of short-term planning back to back, that way the long-term planning will take care of itself.

THE DOOM LOOP

Never put capacity ahead of demand. As a new business, it is tempting to get overexcited at the first flourish of consumer interest. Don't fall into the trap of expanding capacity to fulfil demand. Capacity should always follow demand, never the other way around.

OMAR M. ALMAHMOUD

CEO of ICT Fund

A s CEO of the ICT Fund, Omar Almahmoud has been recognised as one of the youngest leaders in the UAE's public sector. And, under his direction, the ICT has become the main investing agency behind the UAE's Astronauts Programme, the Mars 2117 Initiative and the Emirates Lunar Mission. He regards himself, not merely a businessperson, but "a symbol - an emblematic figure representing what could be achieved when someone from the UAE dared to dream beyond the horizons set up by societal norms."

It's almost inconceivable that Omar's role today is to push forward technological innovations and space missions, when his family didn't have the necessities like electricity growing up.

Their generation grew up sleeping on rooftops and pouring water over themselves to keep cool. Now they are "planning the next iteration of human presence on a different celestial body." For Omar, "the work [he does] is a representation of whom [he is]." And his work today entails leading the ICT Fund, a public development fund with the purpose of building a "knowledge-based society in the UAE, focused primarily on the ICT sector. It has four investment pillars; education, research & development, incubation and entrepreneurship."

"EVERYONE IS THE SON OR DAUGHTER
OF THEIR ENVIRONMENT, MORE THAN
THEY ARE OF A SET PARENT."

YOU ARE WHERE YOU COME FROM

Omar is a great believer in people being shaped by their environment. His family has a background in education that began in 1905, and from then, every generation went on to become "either scholars, judges, or setting up free schools in the region." His grandparents were both well-known judges and scholars, and his parents went on to study abroad and become professors; his father in political science and his mother in education. This strong academic upbringing has provided him with a foundation that he leans on to this day.

The joy of "tinkering with electronics and computers" came early to Omar, and he remembers having PCs in the family home as early as the 1980s, sparking in him a love for technology. He eventually became torn between three possible career paths. He loved to draw, which attracted him to a career in architecture, but he was also interested in computer engineering and telecommunications. So, he applied for all three subjects at different universities, and got accepted to each course. His decision-making had a strong pragmatic element, and when he found that there was only one university in the region which offered telecommunication degrees, he accepted that particular course in the belief that "being a rare commodity was a way to elevate your market status once you graduated."

THE ENTREPRENEUR

Omar's final year project brief was to create a smart home system. He programmed a circuit board which was connected to a live building, and through a voice activated system, instructions like turning on the air-conditioning, or opening garage doors, and working appliances could be fulfilled. He explains, "I was extremely inspired standing on stage, presenting this live demonstration for the whole university to see." Telecommunications had just got exciting for Omar.

Encouraged by this confidence boost, Omar took a different route to most of his peers after graduating in 2007 and, instead of seeking employment, began pursuing investment for his first venture as an entrepreneur. His company, Esal - Building Life with Technology, specialised in mobile applications and solutions such as SMS, MMS and Bluetooth technologies.

He then went on to found a number of organisations: smsPages.ae featured a new web.20 concept, placing classified advertisements online by SMS.Dubai Tech Nights, the largest tech meetup group in the UAE. Ubuntu's UAE's Local Community and The Intellect, a website dedicated to curated articles selected from life, psychology, business and self-improvement. X Artificial Intelligence, a company that uses only AI as its workforce. Furthermore, he is a member of many boards, and for the past eleven years, has been at the helm of an organisation which strives to promote entrepreneurship in the UAE ICT sector.

THE POWER OF NETWORKING

Omar was considered "a poster boy for UAE nationals to be entrepreneurs." And was invited to many events to talk about entrepreneurship and setting up companies. He began building a network of mentors with accomplished individuals who were extremely successful in their careers. One of his mentors was the VP of Motorola, and he was responsible for research and development of their 13 R&D centres globally. Omar was eventually invited to join his team, as Manager of technology investments when his mentor moved to a new role as CTO at Dubai Silicon Oasis. Omar's role was specifically to set up incubation centres and support entrepreneurs with incentives, programs and initiatives.

It was an opportunity for Omar, but also left him in a quandary. He left his start-up role, and accepted the opportunity, working for Dubai Silicon Oasis Authority for about two years. He gained a lot of exposure and experience, explaining, "our vision was to support the ecosystem in terms of technology and start-ups and engineers and working with local universities and attracting overseas companies who have technology and know how to be based in Dubai."

Omar's tenure at Dubai Silicon Oasis Authority ended abruptly, as the CTO team left due to conflicting strategies with the management of the authority, but this led to another opportunity for Omar, and he joined the ICT fund, a move that "catapulted" his career.

ONE SINGLE NUMBER

Omar suggests that a big part of being an effective leader is the ability to make timely decisions, and data is key in providing that necessary information quickly. "You'd be surprised how many people in business leadership roles don't have enough data for them to call the shots immediately, or to pre-emptively take decisions." He proposes that data should be presented as a single metric and demonstrates this with an example of how the new British Airways terminal was set up to have live information on planes leaving on time, planes leaving late, luggage, staff, customers, water control and everything in between using "one single number which is a representation of everything working harmoniously together."

A second part of being an effective leader according to Omar is "mindfulness, not from a Stoic perspective, but actually having your mind occupied with the task in hand." He suggests that having your mind fully focused "optimises the quality of your decision."

Doing business in both New York and Dubai has brought up some interesting comparisons regarding processes and approaches. He notes that New York has a set way of "doing finances" and so is more stringent, whereas "Dubai is a hub for diverse nationalities, so there's a fusion of different approaches, schools and mindsets."

GREAT EXPECTATIONS

For Omar, having great expectations and optimism for the future is "almost a self-fulfilling prophecy." So far, under his leadership, the ICT Fund has funded the moon rover, an astronaut programme and put an astronaut in the International Space Station. But he insists that the organisational route is to follow in a similar plan, with the "ultimate purpose of expanding [their] presence locally and over this planet."

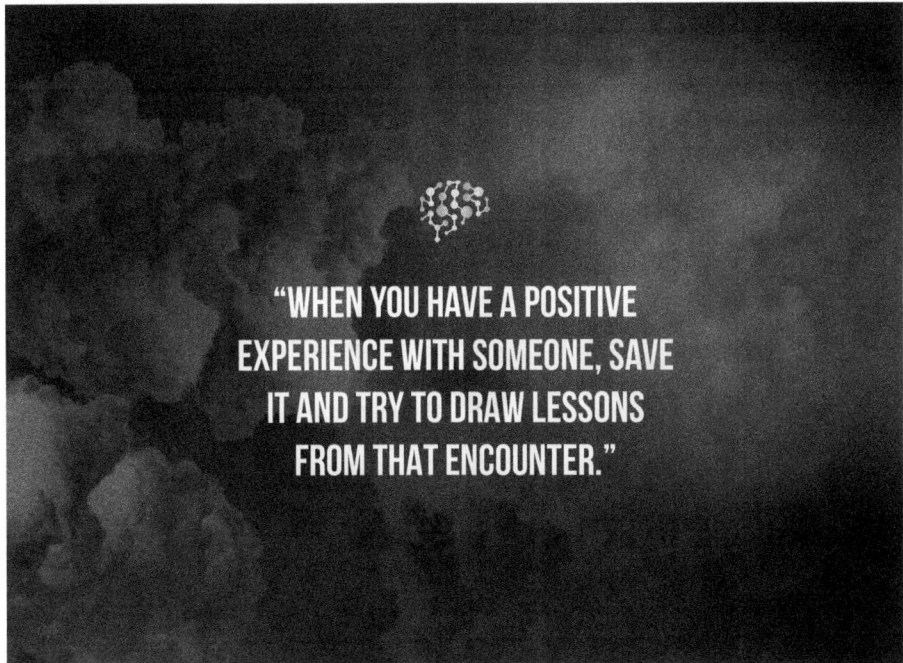

"WHEN YOU HAVE A POSITIVE EXPERIENCE WITH SOMEONE, SAVE IT AND TRY TO DRAW LESSONS FROM THAT ENCOUNTER."

ABUNDANCE

Omar has a unique attitude towards business and suggests "we approach building businesses with an abundant mindset." He offers the UAE and Dubai as prime examples of how approaching something from a level of abundance creates positive outcomes. For instance, they have an attitude of "the more, the merrier" towards immigration, with 90% of the population originating from other places around the world. He also believes that goodness begets good things, arguing that "good deeds and respect will be reciprocated, both in life and business. Somehow, somewhere down the line, it will come back to you."

SELF-IMPROVEMENT

Omar suggests that in today's market, especially with the introduction of AI, your unique selling point is "your creativity, innovation, and intellectual output, and that can manifest itself in work, through projects or initiatives and new responsibilities." His advice is to refine yourself as an individual, through thought leadership, ensuring people want to hear what you have to say. "Intellectual capacity should shine, and if it doesn't shine, you should then start to work on it, start with reading about abstract concepts or ways to improve yourself."

He suggests, apart from reading, writing

A

is another way to refine your way of thinking, and make your mind sharper, "it's the equivalent of the mind's sharpener, and forces you to distil information which you have just read."

Omar recommends that you keep a pen and notebook nearby to write down "fleeting notes or ideas," to elevate your way of thinking. "It would dramatically increase your clarity, to perceive ideas and concepts, especially artwork."

Keeping an open mind is also important, and Omar sets aside one hour every day to meet with someone who he has never met before. He has a link through LinkedIn which automatically books a Zoom session, and he can discuss various topics daily with people from all different backgrounds, giving wide-ranging perspectives, allowing Omar to widen his view. It also grows a network organically.

He feels privileged to experience an "extraordinary entrepreneurial journey, fuelled by continuous learning, meaningful interactions and the opportunities the digital era brings.

"EVERY ENCOUNTER YOU HAVE IS AN OPPORTUNITY."

DUBAI
BUSINESS
LEADERS

DR NAIM MAADAD

CHIEF EXECUTIVE & FOUNDER
OF GATES HOSPITALITY

"Everyone should be responsible for their own destiny, and aspire to change their lives, their family's lives and their community.
Take charge, make a plan, surround yourself with amazing people who will add value to your journey in life, and take care of your mental health, because life is a beautiful journey."

SHAMAILA NAWAZ

CEO of Small Steps Big Dreams

W hen Shamaila Nawaz's 3-year-old son was diagnosed with autism, events in her life began to change. What she didn't realise then was that things would change for the better. Swapping her role as a housewife for the world of business, she became an entrepreneurial educator, supporting children with special educational needs.

Her son's diagnosis in the UK spurred her into action. He responded well to nine months of Applied Behaviour Analysis (ABA), an intervention process founded in the science of learning and behaviour. So Shamaila took her first-hand experience and returned to Dubai to open up her first ABA centre with GEMS Metropole School.

Today, Small Steps Big Dreams provides boundless opportunities for children to live full and happy lives in a society that often overlooks their potential. Small Steps was nominated for the GESS Educational Awards (2020) and was also featured in a documentary, 'I Am Determined,' which was shortlisted at the Toronto Film Festival and won the Audience Choice Award (2021).

She is proud to admit that her biggest achievement remains the countless parents who can see their children flourish because of the work of Small Steps. It is also a special bonus to see that her son, who is now 11 years old, is also flourishing because of a determined mother who refused to give up. She claims he has been her biggest influence, "I have learned so much from him."

"TO BE A LEADER, YOU HAVE TO BE FEARLESS, SELFLESS, AND BE ABLE TO FACE RESISTANCE."

THE START OF SMALL STEPS

"You don't tend to take much notice of things like autism until it affects your own child. However, when my little boy was diagnosed, I started to realise just how difficult it was to get him the right help." Shamaila's story really starts when she wasn't able to get her son accepted to any schools because they didn't have the resources to support him. "I knew I wasn't the only one with a child on the spectrum, so I felt I needed to explore the possibilities, not just for my own son but for other children as well."

Along with her business partner, who has a background in education, Shamaila approached GEMS Metropole, a substantial educational group in the UAE. She spoke with the Head of Inclusion, "who loved the concept," and in 2016, they opened up a centre within the school to provide ABA therapy to children with learning difficulties.

It is an individual centre within the school, so they can support the children within the mainstream school environment. She explains that "this part is extremely important because children on the spectrum already feel very isolated, so it's necessary to be part of the school and access its curriculum." It's also more convenient for the parents.

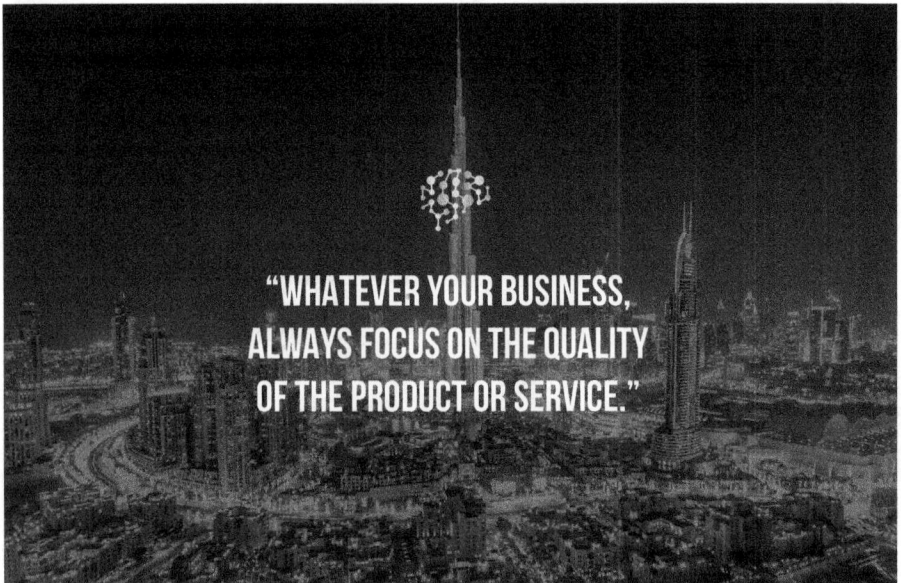

"WHATEVER YOUR BUSINESS, ALWAYS FOCUS ON THE QUALITY OF THE PRODUCT OR SERVICE."

Shamaila now has two branches of Small Steps in partnership with GEMS Founders schools. She knew she could only work with schools that were understanding and supportive. "It's been great working with their Principal and founder, Mr Matthew Burfield. He's been very supportive of us since day one and always says that Small Steps Inclusion is a very special initiative for him. It's important to us that those on board are involved out of empathy for the children rather than as just another box ticking exercise."

THE CHALLENGES

It hasn't all been plain sailing, and there have been a number of challenges and obstacles Shamaila has had to overcome. There were obvious difficulties when schools closed during the pandemic, and it was especially hard for centres like Small Steps. Unlike mainstream schools, where they were able to change their teaching methods to online with relative ease, children on the spectrum did not respond as well to change, disruption, or the independence required for this type of learning and teaching. "We knew that consistency was really important to the children and that they just didn't respond well to distance learning, so I opened up my home as an alternative."

Shamaila felt obliged to fulfil her obligations to parents but also her obligation to continue therapies for the children, who would soon "regress" without them. So, her house was converted into a makeshift therapy centre. "I moved all my furniture and made the room downstairs into a nursery, and a lot of parents opened their own homes as well." It was a tough call, with the added pressure of parents not being able to pay because they themselves weren't being paid during lockdown.

Financial instability was not new to Shamaila, since she and her partner absorbed costs before the business was established. "It has also been really expensive to open the centres because of the resources required, and the way things are done in Dubai. You can't just open a centre like this to create business, it's a vocation that requires love, affection, and strategic planning."

Apart from finances, and relocating the centre to her home, as a mother to a little boy also on the spectrum, she had the added stress of looking after him and attending to his anxieties surrounding the drastic change to his routine. "They need to be entertained all the time because they don't know what to do with themselves, so you need to tell them when to move on to another activity."

No matter what challenges she has faced, Shamaila is a natural problem-solver. When the governing body in Dubai only allowed children to start school at the age of three, Shamaila knew they could get diagnosed early, so she started an early intervention programme to prepare them for the school transition. She has recently opened a centre at Jebel Ali Village Nursery, an achievement she's really proud of.

THE POSITIVES

"When I think back to the children who arrived at Small Steps not even being able to sit in a classroom and are now all thriving in mainstream schools without support, it's extremely rewarding."

Working with GEMS has obviously been a positive experience for Shamaila, allowing her to establish herself as one of the main players in this field. The collaboration has offered students the full school experience. For example, "a lot of our children can't do simple tasks like sit on a school bus, and GEMS loans us empty buses, so the children can experience sitting on a bus with other children. That way, they can be included in activities like field trips." She realises that it takes a lot of empathy and understanding, "and not all schools would do this, so it's made a big difference."

"We also have a great partnership with the inclusion team at GEMS Founders School, they have really helped and supported us." They advise Shamaila on the best classes for the students to attend because she is dealing with a wide range of needs. They also exchange school reports, which come together to produce a more complete and detailed report on each individual child. It's a collegial process that takes a holistic approach.

She now gets people from all over the world coming to Small Steps for the specific provisions she offers "because they can't find this level of help elsewhere in Saudi Arabia, Europe, or even Britain." She confidently says that after six years in business, Small Steps is one of the top inclusion facilities in the UAE. "There are no other centres supporting children with the same quality of therapy within a mainstream setting. We survived the challenges, and now we're flourishing."

THE FUTURE FOR SMALL STEPS

The success of Small Steps has really been down to Shamaila's commitment to keeping it a high-quality experience for both parents and their children. "My selling point is that children are going to get everything my own child is getting - and I guarantee that." The way she is able to guarantee this is by keeping Small Steps - small, "I don't want to open 100 centres, but only a few, and that should keep the quality high." However, with the proper training in place, Shamaila is also open to franchise opportunities.

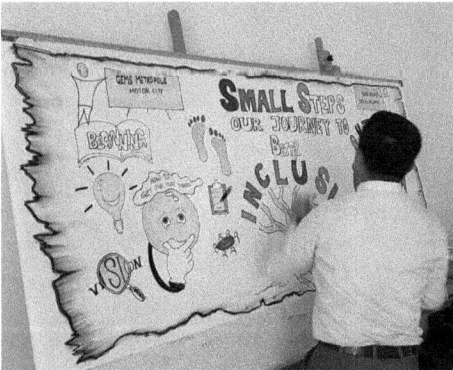

After placing provisions in schools and nurseries, Shamaila really wanted to start responding to the needs of older children on the spectrum. She was getting a lot of enquiries about supporting teenagers with alternative and non-conventional pathways so that they too are able to fully participate in society and live happy, healthy, and productive lives.

"With autism and other conditions, issues can sometimes develop as children grow. To provide support in this area, we're looking at vocational training, and we already provide nanny training that's very popular here in Dubai. Hospitality is also huge in this region, so there'd be lots of opportunities for vocational training in this field - it's certainly on our to-do list."

She explains that the structure at Small Steps is quite hierarchical. At the top, there's the Board Certified Behaviour Analyst (BCBA). "There are very few of them globally, so they're quite expensive to have on the payroll." Then there are the supervisors, and Registered Behaviour Technicians (RBT) who actually deliver the programmes to the children. "For each child on our programme, there's a dedicated, trained therapist who remains with them throughout. It's all quite bespoke, complex, and expensive, but it's important for us to focus more on the quality of provision than the quantity."

"THE KEY TO SUCCESS IS TO HAVE THE COURAGE TO KEEP GOING, EVEN IN THE FACE OF ADVERSITY OR SETBACKS, BECAUSE SUCCESS IS NOT A ONCE IN A LIFETIME ACHIEVEMENT AND FAILURE IS NOT A DEAD END."

Shamaila is aware that there is "still a cultural stigma in the region" and that it takes time for local parents to accept a diagnosis and seek help. Nevertheless, she does have a lot of demand in Abu Dhabi and will be opening a centre there soon before focusing on her long-term plans in Qatar and Saudi Arabia.

DOING BUSINESS IN DUBAI

Shamaila advises that to do business in Dubai, you need to understand the personality of the place and how it works, and that process takes time. "The administration and laws here are very unique and very different from most places, but once you understand Dubai a little, it becomes a platform for opportunities."

She believes there is a misconception about Dubai that "money grows on trees and everything is made of gold. It's a wonderful place, and you do get a lot of opportunities, but you also get disappointments, so you need to be realistic."

Shamaila has lived in Pakistan and spent most of her life in the UK, and of all the places she has lived and visited, "Dubai is by far the most amazing. Especially as a woman, I feel very safe, and it's secure for children too."

She is keen to contest the stereotype of how women are viewed and treated in Arab countries, claiming that in Dubai, "women

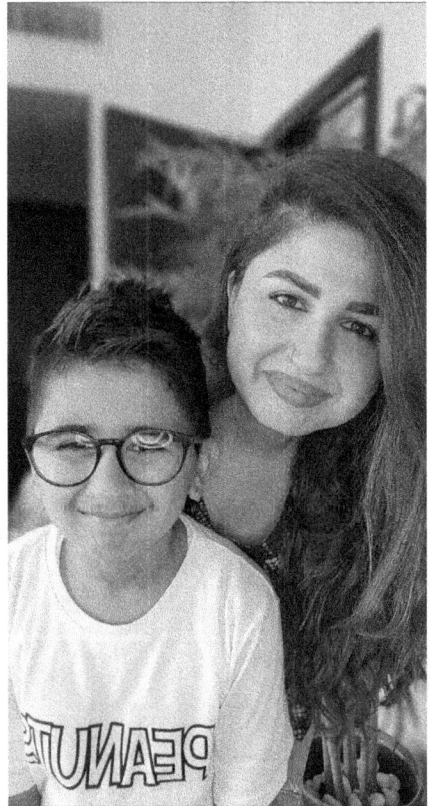

get recognition, respect, love, and attention," pointing out that there are laws to protect women and there's no gender pay gap. "Pay is directly linked to merit, regardless of gender." In fact, a recent study placed the UAE first out of 132 countries for treating women with respect. There's no place quite like Dubai.

"Dubai has given me a lot. I feel like it has allowed me to leave my son a legacy. I've been able to thrive here and do something that, I feel, is very noble. Furthermore, I love my work and love when parents tell me how much their child is progressing, and how they have entered mainstream education purely because of Small Steps. This work is therapy for me."

Shamaila feels lucky to have her family living with her in Dubai and to have that important support system in place. "My dad is someone I really look up to and always consult with when I face any challenges in life. He gives me the best advice, and I have learned a lot from his life experiences and wisdom."

HOW CAN THE WORLD CHANGE FOR THE BETTER?

As a Muslim, Shamaila has recently taken up early morning prayer. She started it during Ramadan and feels it gives her a sense of peace and that it has changed her own world for the better, even in a small sense. "There's still so much judgement and negativity, both in real life and on social media, and that really needs to change. My best friend and business partner has a motto: 'Always be curious, not judgmental.' One way the world could change for the better is if people just let each other live, because you never know what challenges others are facing."

She also believes that another thing that could change the world for the better "would be to get rid of the stigma around disabilities and learning difficulties." For Shamaila, the world would be a much better place if people were always humble toward others and more accepting of children and adults on the spectrum.

DUBAI
BUSINESS
LEADERS

"Always go with an attitude of fusion, of taking different sources to come up with your idea. Look at multiple approaches and fuse the best together. Diverse ideas can come together to create a bigger idea."

Mido Chishty
CMO - Your Marketing Chief Ltd

"Grow through what you go through. If we all learn to grow a little stronger from the challenges we experience, we will all be in for a beautiful surprise."

Charul Jaitly
International Keynote Speaker, Published Author & Winner
of Mrs UAE International 2021

"As we all navigate a very uncertain, external landscape in our businesses, we are faced with many challenges from climate change to economic insecurities, to poverty and so much more. Therefore, we must ensure that we put purpose and impact in the forefront of all our actions. And we must transform our mindset to one which is bold, aspirational and disruptive, because only through innovation and collaboration will we be able, as business leaders, to contribute to making our world a better place."

Noha Hefny
Founder and CEO - People of Impact

"Before you take on a role or an initiative, always make sure you know who you are dealing with, and the dynamics you will be facing."

Rafael Goncalves
Experienced C-Level Leader, Board Advisor,
Growth Strategist, Angel Investor & Coach

PEGAH GOL

Executive Board Member &
Investor in AI talent platform, Serial Entrepreneur,
Keynote Speaker, C-Suite Branding Advisor

As an award-winning entrepreneur and 8 times bestselling author, Pegah Gol has used her extensive experience in the recruitment industry to help jobseekers climb that career ladder and find success. Since graduating in 2004, she has been heavily involved in talent acquisition, has been a Headhunter for top-level management executives and has also achieved a degree from The School of Fashion and Design in Milan in 2016. Her success didn't stop there and in the same year, she founded Glasswing Consulting based in Dubai. And, as CEO, she is offering executive personal branding to c-level executives and entrepreneurs.

With numerous business titles, Pegah has also obtained a number of prestigious awards, including "Top 50 Marketing Influencers to Follow" and the Gold STEVIE Award for "Business Influencer of the Year", demonstrating how she is building an incredible career legacy in Dubai and across the world.

It seems a long time since she first arrived in the city looking for work. But Dubai, as usual, has delivered, and with hard work, perseverance and vision, Pegah is a gleaming example of what Dubai can offer. Whilst her Instagram posts show the allure of catwalk poses and pretty dresses, set against the extravagance of Milan and Dubai's gorgeous landscapes, underneath there stands an astute and formal businesswoman with serious things to say, especially when it comes to human rights, gender equality and the environment.

"THE FIRST STEP IS ALWAYS
THE MOST CRUCIAL ONE,
DESPITE THE DIFFICULTIES
THAT COME WITH IT."

PEGAH THE AUTHOR

As a child, books opened up an entire new world for Pegah. When she read, she was immediately transported to unfamiliar lands, in different times, and she would engage with diverse people from all over the world. Like most self-confessed bookworms, it has always been her aspiration to write her own book.

With seven years experience in recruitment and having interviewed over 12,000 people, she felt qualified enough to impart some of her knowledge to help others achieve their professional goals. Although she felt accomplished enough in career advice, she wasn't confident whether her writing skills were up to the job. So, she enrolled in a writing course, and her debut book was published in 2020. 'The Formula' is Pegah's sought after guide to finding a job the modern way and collates all the top secrets of the recruitment industry, professional CV writing techniques and technology tools for easier job hunting.

Pegah feels fortunate to have her book published right before the pandemic, as her intention behind writing her book was to help all jobseekers during the challenging time and the pandemic was one of those. Obviously, the recruitment industry had taken a downwards turn during that period, but being the entrepreneur she is, she viewed it as an opportunity to concentrate on fulfilling her mission through her book. "I believe that being an author gives you a level of authority, whether you are writing fiction or nonfiction, you can change people's lives. I see authorship as my legacy."

RECRUITMENT AND THE GENDER DIVIDE

With a passion for human rights, Pegah holds particularly strong views on the empowerment of women. As an executive board member on the Global Women Leaders Committee, she has spoken at public events about gender equality, entrepreneurship, technology and innovation, and she holds the belief that "there are still barriers and potential challenges for women, especially in business." She proposes that women shouldn't be competing with men as "it serves no purpose." Instead, she feels that women need to accept that men and women are different, "we both have different skill sets, different powers, and different behaviours." Pegah suggests that empowering women is all about securing equal rights, and that women need to be confident in who they are and understand that they are, indeed, enough. "They must believe in the power they have within themselves." She explains that she is aware of her own power, and this understanding has opened doors for her without having to fight for it. This sense of self-empowerment and inner confidence was paramount in getting others to take her seriously, receiving promotions and achieving her goals.

As a veteran in the recruitment industry, Pegah has observed first-hand other recruiters favouring men over women or hiring based on nationality. She maintains an awareness of bias and refuses to participate, praising Dubai as a "melting pot of over 200 nationalities where everyone is treated equally, regardless of gender or nationality." Interestingly, AI technology is at the forefront of non-discriminatory recruitment processes. It does not select candidates based on gender, ethnicity, age, or region, but purely on suitability for the position, hence providing the best outcome for the employer and prospective employee.

DUBAI AND WOMEN ENTREPRENEURS

Pegah's role as a board member of the Global Women Leaders Committee, is to remind everyone that "women can be empowered and all of them can flourish together." In Dubai, women have many facilities to encourage personal growth and empowerment; there are forums and

committees through the expat community, as well as government initiatives. Each year on 28th August there is the Emirati Women's Day. Founded in 2015 by Her Highness Sheikha Fatima bint Mubarak, it serves to recognise Emirati women's value and contribution to their country and to recognise the importance of equality.

Safety has never been a concern for Pegah as a woman living and working in Dubai. She feels it is "a city where you can feel free and secure," and expresses how "people who live and move here all share a common goal, one of pride, support and overall self-improvement." Pegah holds the belief that her future in Dubai was destiny. From the day of her arrival in the city, to her first job as a customer assistant and onto her current success as an author, entrepreneur, coach, and businesswoman, she feels it was meant to be. Rather modestly, she maintains that she did little in this journey, "I just followed the path, and am extremely proud that I've helped thousands of people to find work."

DOING BUSINESS IN DUBAI

She now regards the UAE as her "adoptive country," as it provides all the necessary facilities and amenities conducive to building a thriving business. "I truly believe that if you are going to succeed, you will succeed in Dubai." She is keen to express that the cultural diversity of the city provides opportunities for personal and professional growth. At one time, Pegah was working alongside people from 20 different nationalities, which exposed her to different cultures, and is something she considers "essential when trading on an international platform." She explains that this is a crucial aspect that many overlook, "especially here in Dubai, and that puts them at a distinct disadvantage in relation to those who go the extra mile."

PRACTICE FOR SUCCESS

Pegah advises that different successful people adopt different routines for success, and that one size doesn't fit all. She finds that meditation works well for her, and it's something she practices twice a day. "I find it facilitates focus and clears the mind." Like many other very busy and successful people, she likes to be organised, and so sets out her intentions and plans for the day ahead. "Mindset too is important. For example, adopting a more relaxed, willing attitude rather than a more pressurised 'must do' stance."

THE FUTURE IN DUBAI

Over the 15 years Pegah has spent in Dubai, she has witnessed many changes, and only sees "good things happening here in the years to come." She identifies the Museum of the Future as a prime example, "whilst most museums look back on the past, Dubai always looks towards the future, and that's exciting."

On her own future in Dubai, Pegah is optimistic and confident that she will continue to flourish in what she feels promises to be one of the most advanced countries in the world over the next decade. She will continue to embrace technology and fully intends to keep pace with all that is to come, comparing it to the 1980s, when computers were still in their infancy and the concept of mobile phones were still far in the future.

FOR THE LOVE OF TECH

Pegah intends to take advantage of whatever future technology brings and to use it as a positive tool in improving the world of work. She is

accepting that the future will continue to offer advances in the realms of robots and AI, and her strategy is to work with this, not against it. Her recommendation is that we "hone our skills and use this technology to improve our work patterns and use it to make life easier."

While some see innovation as a threat to jobs, Pegah is more upbeat and positive. Although she recognises the potential challenges, she believes that it will ultimately serve us well. Pegah is keen to highlight all the many jobs that technology has created, citing social media and influencing as just one example. Further, she reminds us that we can use voice recognition to send messages around the world in a matter of minutes, even seconds. "When we accept this positively, we can use it to improve our own work/ life balance, not least by using the extra time technology affords us to do things we actually enjoy – to have free, quality time away from our desks."

With her obvious love of technology as a tool for self-improvement, she still feels that "we need to interact and communicate with one another – this is something not possible (yet) for robots to execute for us." She uses the example of sales, as an industry where personal contact is vital.

And what about the issue of creativity? AI can produce stunning art, illustrations and images in a matter of seconds. To this, Pegah argues that "a robot can do this, but it cannot come from our own hearts and convey our own deep, personal feelings. There is no inspiration and emotion there that can tell our story for us, as we would ourselves."

ON THE FUTURE

With confidence in the future and a forward-thinking attitude, Pegah wants us to collectively focus more on environmental issues. She speaks with knowledge on the subject, and praises Dubai's current strategies and policies, lending weight to the assertion that the city is planted firmly in the future. Regarding the use of plastics, she

wants to see more solutions for recycling and cleaning our oceans. "Dubai is going forwards, not backwards and if you are fortunate enough to live [there], nothing is impossible, you just have to believe that you can do it."

LESSON FROM THE PERSONAL BRANDING EXPERT

Pegah introduced the game-changing "The Authority Building Formula™". This pioneering methodology empowers C-Level executives to establish themselves as market thought leaders, magnetising lucrative opportunities, and executive board positions, enhancing their reputation as the go-to experts in their industry with the power of personal branding.

1. We all have something unique within us, don't be afraid to share it with the world.

2. Being an author brings us authority, if you ever dreamt of sharing your expertise, do it either through a book or start by sharing articles.

3. Opportunities are waiting for us, we can only turn them into reality by taking action.

4. Out of your comfort zone is where the magic happens, dare to get out of your comfort zone and create magic in your life.

5. Your story of struggle could be someone else's inspiration and survival guide, don't give up.

> **"IDENTIFYING THE 'WHYS' WILL SAVE YOU TIME AND ENERGY AND WILL GET YOU THE RESULTS YOU ARE LOOKING FOR."**

DUBAI
BUSINESS
LEADERS

LLOYED LOBO

AUTHOR OF 'FROM GRASSROOTS TO GREATNESS'
CO-FOUNDER OF BOAST.AI & TRACTION

"Yesterday's innovation is always tomorrow's commodity. But if you build a community, you won't become a commodity.

Harley-Davidson almost went bankrupt in the 1980s, and rebuilt the company centered on the values of the community, and now it's an iconic brand worth over $7 billion.

Brands of yesterday were built on what they told the world about themselves. Brands of the future will be built on what the community says about them."

LAMEEN ABDUL-MALIK AND TALHA SHAIKH

CEO and Director of Honest Management

L ameen Abdul-Malik and Talha Shaikh are responsible for Honest Management, a consulting company founded by the Nobel Peace Prize Laureate, and CEO, Lameen, and under the directorship of Talha.

As a consulting firm, it offers what many others do; leadership development, digital transformation and IT consulting, government relations, empowering start-ups, thought mapping, keynote speaking, and the list continues. But it's not necessarily what they do that makes them one of the most "respected, reliable and sincere" services in the MENA region, it's how they do it. With a focus on honesty, sincerity, trust, and humility, Honest Management is at the forefront of shifting corporate mindsets. Through their "performance-enhancing advisory service," and with a team of experts in their fields, the consulting firm guides and supports individuals and companies to reach their full potential by re-establishing integrity in the business world.

Honest-Management was born from a passion to create a better world, through generating sustainable and profitable business models which will transform the corporate landscape. It's a thought-provoking concept, which reflects the multifaceted individuals who lead the enterprise.

LAMEEN

In contrast to the consumer-driven ideology that defines most of the developed world, Lameen's dream of being a billionaire isn't focused on financial rewards, but on the concept of creating "a community to impact one billion lives positively." It's an altruistic premise, which is born out of Lameen's innate philosophical stance that "service to others is the rent you pay for your life here on earth."

The making of Lameen is a long and complex story. Born in Switzerland and of British Nigerian heritage, he was able to fulfil a schoolboy dream when was sent to study in the UK at the age of 12. He eventually went on to study Economics, History and Religious Studies during A-Levels, which sparked in him a passion for solving development problems and poverty by using technology, an endeavour that eventually led him and his colleagues to being awarded the Nobel Peace Prize in 2005.

Now, with decades of business experience behind him, Lameen is driven to help create a shift in the corporate world, from the cold and calculating to the kind and compassionate. Although there are still some business leaders just paying lip service to a new era of 'people before profit', refreshingly, Lameen demonstrates his integrity through acts of philanthropy. One of his proudest moments was when he was allocated approximately $200,000 of the Nobel Peace Prize to establish Zambia's first cancer hospital, which now treats about 1,500 cancer patients each year. An astonishing legacy which will continue to directly save lives, and a prime example of how Lameen likes 'to pay it forward'.

With an MBA in International Management, his experience has been wide and varied, and has taken him around the world, from working at the International Trade Department in London, to the International Atomic Energy Agency in Vienna, and from working as the Managing Director of his café in South Africa to being head hunted to lead thought leadership at a Think Tank in Saudi Arabia. For the past few years, Lameen has been based in Dubai, where he launched his 100 Ideas Café project, a crowdsourcing platform to generate ideas to impact our World. Making a positive difference in the world is a running theme in Lameen's career to date. He's contributed to developing policy on how trade can help poor countries and has used nuclear science and technology to help developing countries address poverty

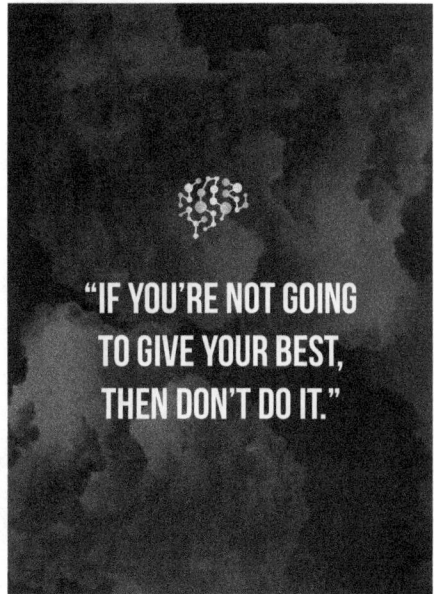

"IF YOU'RE NOT GOING TO GIVE YOUR BEST, THEN DON'T DO IT."

challenges. As the senior project manager for the International Atomic Energy Agency, his remit was to ensure that nuclear science and technology benefited Africa from a political, social and economic perspective.

As a keen connoisseur of coffee, Lameen pursued one of his dreams when he moved his young family from Europe to South Africa to launch Escape Caffé with the ethos of, "serving the best coffee experience in Cape Town." Although his online platform, 100 Ideas Café, is less about coffee and more about the power of exchanged ideas, his true coffee enthusiasm is taken seriously by those who follow his blog 'fromcoffeewithlove.' He has attended many conferences on coffee, and read numerous books on the topic, and, today, could now be considered an expert. He has featured on CNN's website for Drinking Coffee in 2020, and was invited by the International Coffee Organisation to participate in an EU Coffee Symposium with the giant leaders in the coffee world to explore how Africa can benefit from the value chain.

Lameen's intellectual philanthropy continues with his newest venture, Honest Management. Founded at the back end of 2019, the company encapsulates all that Lameen holds dear, and pledges to bring about a shift in the paradigm by making a positive impact on how humans behave in business. Lameen would be the first to acknowledge the talented team he has, which spans across a multitude of fields including, renewable energy, radiotherapy, technology, business growth, international diplomacy, youth development, operations, mind-mapping and organisational behaviour. It reflects the many ways in which Lameen's company can help entities to grow sustainably with a focus on honesty. As CEO, Lameen has found a kindred spirit in Talha Shaikh who, as Director, is passionate about the opportunities which may lay ahead.

DUBAI
BUSINESS
LEADERS

TALHA

Having been born in Saudi Arabia, Talha moved with his family to India at the age of 10 when his father retired. He settled in Mumbai for a number of years, and it was there that his entrepreneurial education truly began, guided by his father and mentor, who pointed him in the right direction. Talha remembers selling mangoes in the suburbs when his father insisted that he should have a return policy. As the 17-year-old attempted to explain that the product was perishable, his father made it clear that "[they] would take full responsibility for what was sold, and the customer should not have to bear the loss due to a flaw in [their] product." Sceptical at first, Talha soon realised that his demonstrable integrity made him instantly popular in the market. He learned the invaluable lesson that remains with him to this day that "taking care of your customer is the best way of taking care of your business."

After obtaining a degree in commerce, Talha moved to Dubai, where he got a number of job offers within the space of a month. Some may say he was simply lucky to find work so quickly, but others might attribute his success to his ability to stand out from

CORPORATE CRICKET LE/

CCL 2022 - SHARJ/

BAHI

Emirates NBD

RAK HOSPITAL

THUMBAY

ADA

UNGER

RCOM

RAMAD

SHAR

"NO ONE CAN LEAD
YOU BETTER THAN
YOURSELF."

the crowd. He explains back then, when CVs were faxed over to HR departments, he instead faxed over a large image of himself with the simple tag "guess who's in town?" He'd thought of everything, even the colour and size of the paper made him stand apart from the rest of the jobseekers.

The result was positive, and Talha began working for a computing consulting start up. With only seven employees at the start, Lattice Computer Consultants grew rapidly into a workforce of over eighty, capturing sixteen countries in multiple markets. His career path was set with a specific focus on "solving business problems through technology." And, after nine successful years as the Marketing Manager, he moved on to directorial roles, always remaining within the UAE, which he now very much considers his home.

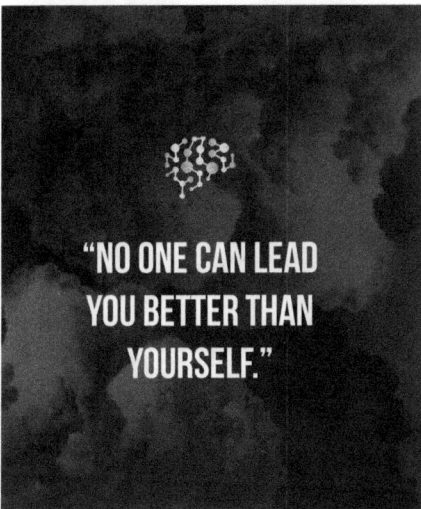

In the spirit of making things happen, Talha got in touch with Lameen through LinkedIn, and a bond formed over a mutual desire to do things honestly in business. Talha explains that he "was very impressed by the fact that somebody had the courage to call their company Honest-Management. The company's name is possibly more significant in Dubai, as Talha warns against too many businesses "lying and pushing to achieve complex solutions." And, after decades immersed in this unscrupulous culture, Talha took a vow of total honesty in 2005. It was a "spiritual decision" which has had many positive benefits, such as "increased business, higher earnings, enhanced reputation, and, perhaps most importantly, a sense of inner peace." He also suggests that "there is no empirical data to prove that dishonesty in business is helping profitability."

It's no surprise that servant leadership is the preferred managerial style for Talha, who suggests that "honesty to yourself, honesty to your shareholders and stakeholders and honesty to your employees" is the key to success. He goes on to ask the perpetual and existential question - "What is the purpose of mankind on this earth?" For Talha, it is to do good, and do no harm. It's this perspective that is gradually drawing in more and more business, from individuals and companies, who are getting tired of the hyperbole and deception.

Talha believes that reputation is everything, and he is proud of the fact that most of their business is obtained by referrals. It's the reputational value of Honest Management that has led Talha to be invited by the Corporate Cricket League to take on the role of President of the Excellence and Fair Play Committee. The gesture is emblematic of how the company is viewed in the business world in Dubai. And, as an example of "doors opening" rather than closing because of honesty, the CCL has also asked the company to "take care of their IT chapter."

Now firmly settled with his family in Dubai, Talha doesn't sense a need to return to Mumbai, which is only a few hours flight away. Dubai has greatly impressed him, and he applauds the leadership for "building a city based on knowledge and consistently

> "WHEN YOU'RE HONEST WITH YOURSELF, YOU CAN EXPLORE MORE ABOUT YOURSELF, AND CHANNEL THAT ENERGY INTO OTHER PEOPLE."

studying the best business practice." Talha suggests that focusing on the infrastructure, such as making the city safe and commuting easy, has attracted "middle-class professionals" who have helped build a thriving and bustling ecosystem. He believes it's a model that can happen anywhere in the world, "as long as the governance is focusing on serving the citizens."

LAMEEN AND TALHA

As CEO and Director of Honest Management, the partners complement each other well. They're united by their passion for doing good, making a positive impact and using technology for the greater benefit. They also provide a 360° service for their clients, covered by their different and extensive areas of expertise, which blend seamlessly. It's not just their good business fit that makes sense, but their easy collaboration, stemming from a shared world view and an uncompromising value system.

The determined duo are walking a path that many will undoubtedly follow in years to come. As consumers become more knowledgeable about transactional processes, there's a possibility that businesses maintaining dishonest practices will be forced to change or become irrelevant. As Lameen rightly points out, "even a dishonest person is keen to do business with an honest person."

"If you chase excellence,
then success will chase you."

Tapan Vaidya
CEO at Papa Johns UAE, KSA & Jordan

"As a leader, you need to create an environment where people feel empowered to reach their full potential. If you allow your people to spread their wings and fly, magic can happen, for them, and for you."

Terry Downes
CEO Mysafe

"Work hard at finding your purpose because that is the one thing that will protect you during times of adversity."

Zohare Haider
Building jalebi.io
#1 Restaurant Inventory Optimizing Technology Company

"Information can either grind you down or polish you up. If you are self-aware, you can use that information to polish yourself, and outperform the rest of the competition."

Casey Cittadino
CEO Athletic Mindset

NINA SEREDAI-UDALOVA

Founder & Managing Director at Ninth Space,
Host of The Brands Through Stories podcast,
Founder of Véa, Entrepreneur

B orn in Kopeysk, Russia, Nina moved to Dubai as a teenager when her parents escaped the struggles of the post-Perestroika era. At that time, 27 years ago, Dubai was an emerging city, very different to the dynamic innovation hub it is today. The city of opportunity has been kind to Nina, who, for the past 19 years, has been involved in numerous successful entrepreneurial endeavours.

Having witnessed the growth and transformation of the UAE, Nina feels proud to have been a part of it. While many come to the country for its luxurious lifestyle, Nina asserts that the UAE has so much more to offer. "With its rich history, visionary leaders, family-oriented culture, and Islamic values, each emirate has its own unique beauty." It is an inspiring place that Nina calls her home today.

As a 'serial entrepreneur', Nina's first business was in conferencing, and she remembers being "one of the first expat women to open an office in Dubai Media City." She was "young, enthusiastic, motivated and fearless," and with those qualities, and the support of her partners in Europe, she organised business conferences aimed at high-level executives working in a wide range of fields such as banking, pharmaceutical, oil and gas, real estate and many others within the Middle East region. This "great job" was the springboard for Nina's entrepreneurial career, and to date, she owns three businesses.

"A TRUE LEADER SEES BEYOND TODAY"

SEES BEYOND TODAY

Nina believes that a "true leader" needs to have certain qualities. Firstly, they need to have a vision and "have the intuition and courage to see beyond today." She's unsure whether these qualities are "inherent in a person or can be learned," but she is certain that it's a rare ability that sets apart the few from the many. Alongside vision, it's necessary to have "focus". Nina suggests that most people are afraid to focus on their vision in case they lose out on other opportunities. Thus, "a true leader believes in his/her vision and can focus on moving towards the vision - no matter what." A third indispensable quality is the ability to "take responsibility". As Nina's work involves working with top executives, she observes that many business leaders are still unprepared to take responsibility and tend to blame their teams for failures. This leads to the fourth quality that Nina believes in - care and empathy. The fifth and final attribute of a good leader is to be a great communicator to empower and engage with people in a way that they will follow you on your journey "through good times and difficult times."

INSPIRING THE CREATION OF MEANINGFUL BRANDS: NINA'S PURPOSE AND BUSINESS JOURNEY.

Nina's purpose in her professional life is to inspire the creation of meaningful businesses - companies with a purpose that positively impact our planet and our lives. It doesn't matter how large or small the impact is, as long as the company is conscious of the impact it wants to make. In order to stay on her path of realising her purpose, she makes sure that all the businesses she owns are connected to it.

Nina's brand strategy and design consultancy has been established in Dubai for 13 years. "It focuses on building meaningful brands that people love and believe in." Ninth Space works across more than 10 countries, catering to middle-sized corporations and large-sized companies, with an impressive list of companies, including the Emirates Group, Majid Al Futtaim, Abu Dhabi University, The Four Seasons, and the governments of Oman and the UAE.

As the founder of Vea (Nina's second company), she wants to help those "who couldn't access [her] services through Ninth Space." Her educational platform aims to inspire and educate entrepreneurs on building brands as a powerful intangible asset of their companies - profitable brands that drive positive change in our world and our society.

One of Nina's recent endeavours is her podcast, "Brands through Stories." Initially developed as a therapeutic tool to regain her confidence after losing her business partner, the podcast has evolved into a passion project that Nina firmly believes in. It strongly connects with her purpose and helps her learn how to succeed in business from other people's experiences. The podcast focuses on the stories of successful entrepreneurs, whose success is measured not solely by their profits but also by their positive impact on the world.

"Having a purpose in my professional life, living it every day and seeing it coming to life through my businesses makes me motivated and empowered and I fall in love with what I do every day".

BRAND STRATEGY

As an expert in brand strategies, Nina suggests that "your brand is everything, your brand is the perception that people have about your company." It is not a marketing tool that is owned by your marketing departments, brand is an intangible asset of the company that can increase the value of your business. "Once

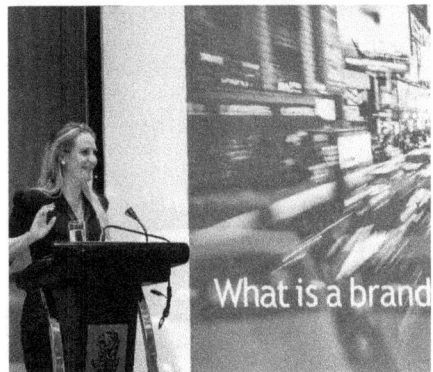

What is a brand

one realises the power of a brand, they can't live without it". Brand Strategy like a business strategy should be the foundation to all brand building. To simplify, it answers five fundamental questions:

1. Who are you as a business?

2. Where are you going?

3. Why are you going there?

4. Who are you doing it for?

5. What makes you unique?

Once a business can answer all the above, "they become much stronger in terms of their focus, clarity and uniqueness." Nina's advice is to focus on your brand strategy before you do anything else in your business because it's ultimately the foundation you will lean on.

I TURNED TO MY PURPOSE TO FIND MY STRENGTH

Like many businesses during COVID, Nina experienced financial upheaval and continual strife. "We had to let everyone go, lost our office after 10 years, had a couple of projects, but no cash in the bank," she recalls. The pressure took its toll, and after 10 years, the partnership was dissolved. Nina found herself on her own, with the sudden reality of having to start from scratch. Lacking belief in herself, she recognised the need for a change in her life. It was during this time that her purpose, "to inspire the creation of meaningful businesses - companies that positively impact our planet and our life" helped her find her strength. "One morning, I woke up realizing that what I do matters to people around me and myself. It keeps me on my path and gives me hope that I'm doing the right thing in life." This realisation rejuvenated Nina's strength and opened doors to new creative opportunities. This is how the podcast "Brands Through Stories" was born. Nina explains that it was her intuition that paved the way: "I knew that to overcome all this insecurity, I needed to do something I hadn't done before—something that was strongly connected to my purpose."

BRANDS THROUGH STORIES

Brands Through Stories was a cathartic outlet for Nina, and one that allowed her to start believing in herself again due to the "long list of friends" who pulled through to participate and share their own stories. For Nina, "it's turned out to be an incredible platform that helps [her] to explore, learn new things and to build up [her] confidence." With her first episode now having reached 150,000+ views, it's not only good for Nina's self-esteem, but also shines a light on "some incredible people and their inspiring stories," who can now share their experiences and wisdom. Nina wants to keep the podcast's authenticity by only inviting special people with big hearts and real stories to tell.

"THERE'S NO FUTURE FOR A GOOD LEADER WITHOUT EMPATHY."

She claims that hosting a podcast is "probably one of the most intimate moments you can have with a guest," under the bright lights and darkened studio, facing each other for "forty minutes to one hour of complete immersive discourse." She gets the whole spectrum of emotions, and each interviewee is a personal source of inspiration for Nina.

OPTIMISM IS IN MY BLOOD

Although Nina likes to read and listen to people's ups and downs, she admits her own life has been quite consistent. Her main motivation is her family and especially her kids. "I want my kids to live in a beautiful and kind world. Having my companies that help a bit in creating that world makes me feel motivated and hopeful that our planet and our kids will have a positive and bright future." Nina is also thankful to her parents, who identified her entrepreneurial spirit early on and sent her to business school. Having a family "who always believed in [her], no matter what," must have been a real source of strength for Nina in difficult times. She claims "optimism is in [their] blood," a quality all successful entrepreneurs must possess.

She also considers herself lucky that her family chose Dubai. At the time, it was a much smaller place with a select number of high-powered executives "earning good money and helping the visionary leaders building the UAE." It was here that Nina rubbed shoulders with professionals from all over the world, and she considers Dubai as her mentor, enjoying being part of the process and witnessing Dubai's transformation from the ground up.

I ENJOY BEING A WOMAN

Nina feels particularly empowered as a woman in Dubai and suggests that women need to embrace their gender and "just enjoy it." She worked with a number of "beautiful, serious, smart, and well-respected women" in the UAE government to help brand the Gender Balance Council—an authority that aims at reducing the gender gap in the country. It was an amazing journey to work with these women who could be a true inspiration for every woman wanting to have a successful career without losing herself as a woman. Contrary to the "misconceptions" and stereotypes, Nina believes that women have a lot of power and respect in the GCC countries because "they don't need to pretend or compete with anyone. They're true women, mothers, and sisters, and they receive a lot of respect." So, for Nina, Dubai is the perfect place to "live her life and enjoy being a woman."

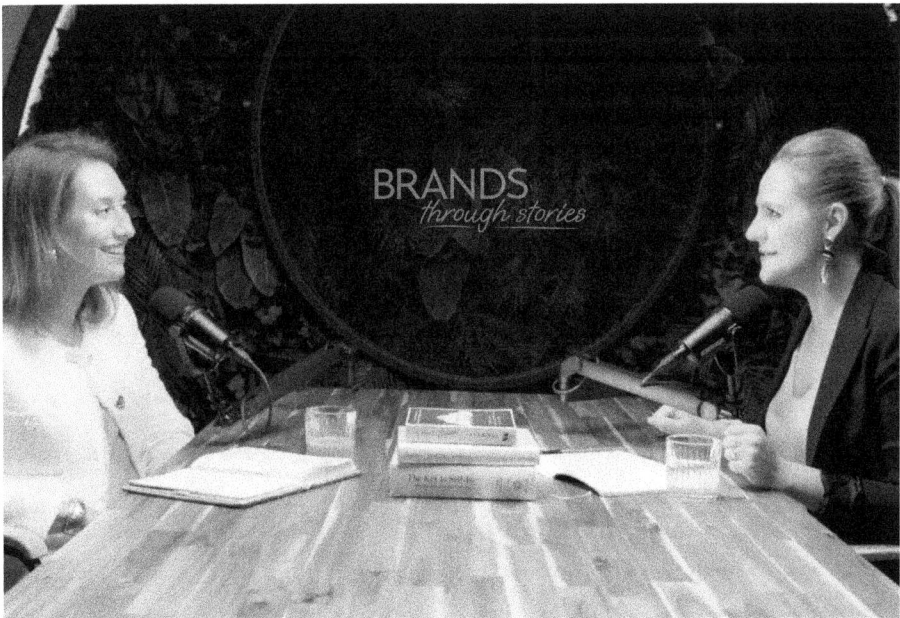

FALL IN LOVE WITH WHAT YOU DO

Having lost her business partner three years ago, Nina has persevered, and now she sees a brighter future for herself. She wants to engage in more speaking opportunities, expand her mentorship programme, introduce more online and offline courses, and publish her book. Her goal is, through all the engagements, to share her message about how building meaningful brands can be both profitable and capable of changing the world for the better.

For Nina, success is subjective and difficult to measure. But she views success as being able professionally to do something she enjoys and believes in whilst living a beautiful and fulfilling life with her loved ones.

A lot of people say that you need to do what you love. Nina believes that if you can't do what you love, then try to "fall in love with what you do, pay attention to small details that excite you, and think about how, through your work, you help other people. Sometimes, your happiness is within your reach, but you can't see it."

"BRAND IS NOT A MARKETING TOOL IT'S A COMPANY'S INTANGIBLE ASSET"

DUBAI
BUSINESS
LEADERS

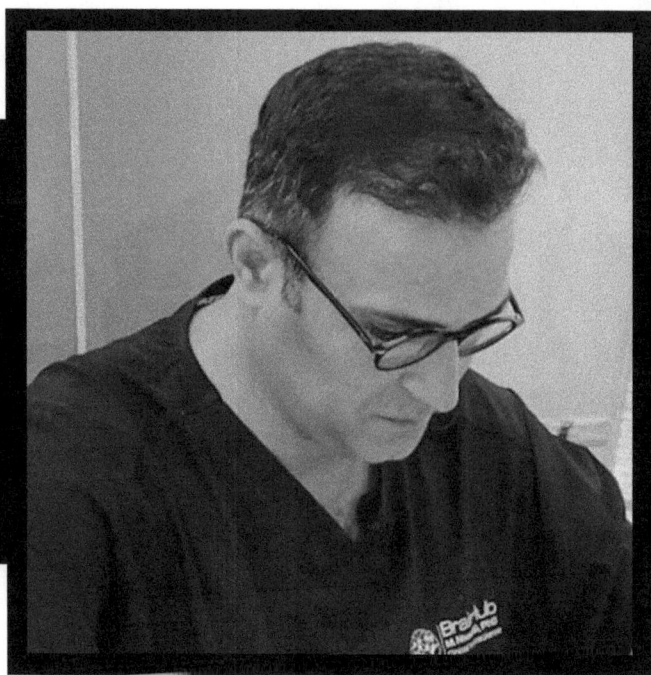

DR MOHAMMAD NAMI

Director at BrainHub UAE, Alumni of the Canadian University, Dubai and
Harvard University, Entrepreneur, TEDx Speaker

B orn in Iran, the young Mohammad grew up with big dreams, a strong academic ability, and a deep fascination with the mysteries of the human brain. After completing his medical degree (MD), he pursued this passion further, focusing on how the brain functions and creates reality for us. After completing his PhD, Dr Nami concluded his clinical fellowship in sleep disorders and then became a Faculty Member and Head of the Department of Neuroscience at Shiraz University of Medical Sciences. He later completed his postgraduate medical education (EWHC) at Harvard Medical School in 2021, where he became an associate member of the alumni.

As a Cognitive Neuroscientist, his work revolves around brain health, neuro-medicine, and sleep health, using neuro-technological advances. Dr Nami uses brain-mapping technologies to look into the brain's chemistry and functional wave patterns in healthy and diseased individuals. His work is his vocation, and he is proud to have contributed to the academic community with his original research work and clinical practice over the past 18 years.

"SLEEP HEALTH IS A KEY PILLAR IN YOUR HOLISTIC HEALTH."

Dr Nami's mission took him to the UAE, where he became the Director of the Brain, Cognition and Behaviour Unit at the BrainHub Polyclinic in Dubai. His main focus today is cognitive and medical neuroscience, particularly cognitive neuropsychology, and the neuroscience of sleep. Firmly believing that mental health and sleep health are intricately connected, Dr Nami is convinced that mental health, brain health and sleep health should be co-promoted, and yet, suggests that sleep is a domain that has been continually overlooked in the medical field. According to Dr Nami, "sleep seems to be the hidden part of the story when we focus on health-related issues."

Currently, Dr Nami is the Assistant Professor in Cognitive Neuroscience and Neuropsychology at the Canadian University Dubai (CUD). He is happy to say that this position gives him "the opportunity to be surrounded by many passionate students and also great scholars and faculty members." For him, being in Dubai, at the Canadian University, offers him a dynamic space to carry out his research and bring more value to his community.

SLEEP

Dr Nami's work focuses on awakening individuals to their "infinite brain and cognitive potential." Through sleep tests, brain mapping and brain health checks, he and his team are involved in clinical processes which employ neurotechnology to improve or empower the brain function. While his expertise mainly falls under sleep health and disorders, as a clinical neuroscientist, he sees a wide range of patients, from those with Alzheimer's disease, dementia, Parkinson's disease, cerebral palsy, motor neuron disease, strokes, and brain trauma, to patients with dysregulated mood, depression, anxiety, PTSD, OCD and phobias. This work also expands into neurodivergent conditions such as ADHD, autism, and even sensory issues, like ultra-low vision or impaired taste and smell.

According to Dr Nami, there are eighty-four different types of sleep disorders. Identifying the type of disorder requires "quantitative, validated metrics and measurements." Polysomnography, a multi-parameter study of sleep, is used as the gold-standard to evaluate sleep-related problems.

DOCTOR IN DUBAI

Having settled in Dubai relatively recently, Dr Nami appreciates the business dynamics and international networking opportunities that the city has to offer, alongside the opportunity to speak with an array of "bright minds and thought leaders," that the region now attracts. It's a hub for innovation, science and technology, so a natural fit for Dr Nami. "Dubai is like a miniature world," full of possibilities. And like many who have made Dubai their home, it's geographically central, so it is easy for him to visit his home country.

Dr Nami finds that Dubai "offers a plethora of opportunities," set in a peaceful atmosphere which allows businesses to run fluidly. "If you want to expand your

business or provide vocational opportunities for others, Dubai is potentially the place to be." Within one year, the BrainHub Polyclinic has gone from opening up a business in 4 or 5 rooms in a tower block, to a beautiful, large villa in one of the most prestigious areas of Dubai. Expanding BrainHub Polyclinic's physical space, and increasing their number of staff practitioners all within a year has been a rewarding challenge, but demonstrates the extent to which Dubai supports innovation and business growth.

THE SLEEP DOCTOR

Scientific research confirms that mental health issues and sleep related problems vary from country to country, and even region to region. Interestingly, Dr Nami and his colleagues have published comprehensive research on the cost of neurological disorders as an economic burden. Specifically concerning sleep disorders, Dr Nami indicates that the Middle-East, South East Asia, India, and Bangladesh have "significantly higher rates of sleep disorders," with as much as over 40% of the population suffering from some sort of sleep ailment. Whereas, in the western world, for example, North America, sleep disorders seem to affect around 10-23% based on community research findings.

Looking at the root cause of sleep disorders, Dr Nami finds that limited physical activity, poor lifestyle habits, depression and anxiety are among the most common causes for sleep problems. Furthermore, lack of sleep is known to be linked to the progression of dementia and Alzheimer's disease.

It's not merely a matter of not being able to sleep, although getting to sleep and staying asleep is an issue, it's the quality of sleep that has the most impact physiologically. Sleep disordered breathing, snoring, pauses in breathing and sleep fragmentation all result in limited airflow, and drops in oxygen levels, which directly, and negatively impact brain function the following day. "This is an ongoing pathology, which puts people at higher risk of developing dementia, memory impairment and ultimately Alzheimer's disease."

Fascinatingly, Dr Nami also identifies older women as being more predisposed to sleep disorders, but, also, more specifically, middle-aged, overweight men with short necks, as they tend to be the group who snore the most.

SLEEP HYGIENE

Sleep hygiene means following a set of common-sense recommendations to maintain proper sleep quantity and quality. Nevertheless, Dr Nami indicates that common-sense isn't that common, and identifies business leaders as being one of the main groups who have poor sleep hygiene. For example, "they tend to sleep less, be more active, and ultimately exchange their business outcomes with their sweet slumber."

In many instances, the proactive approach of many business leaders, according to Dr Nami, is not necessarily sustainable and makes them more prone to burnout. Basically, those who don't get enough sleep, will eventually succumb to the consequences of low cognitive ability and poor functionality which will in turn, affect "their attention, memory, reasoning, planning, decision-making and problem-solving." Most people are also aware that poor sleep can lead to low moods, but for business people, this is even more crucial as a "regulated mood" is imperative when dealing with colleagues, clients and employees.

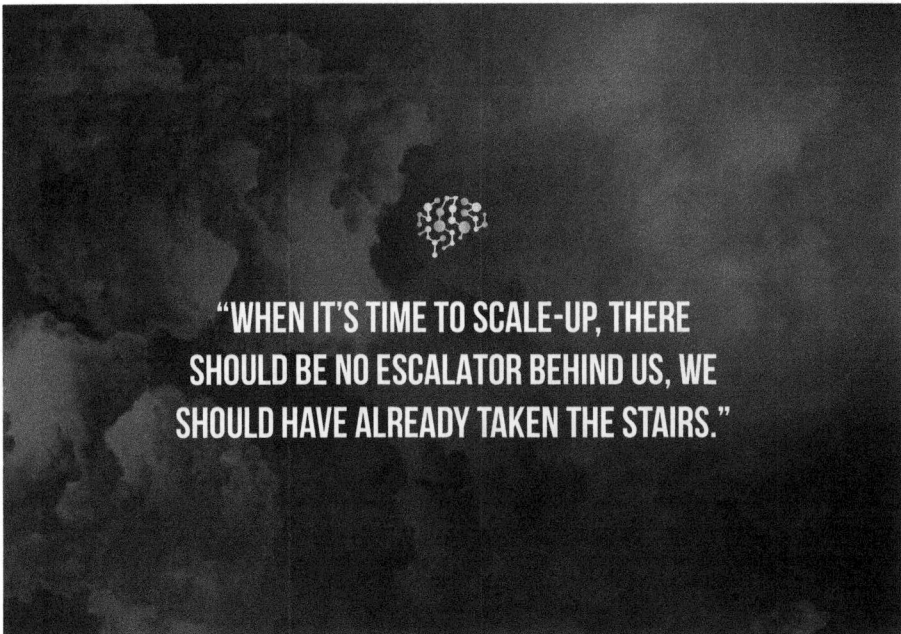

"WHEN IT'S TIME TO SCALE-UP, THERE SHOULD BE NO ESCALATOR BEHIND US, WE SHOULD HAVE ALREADY TAKEN THE STAIRS."

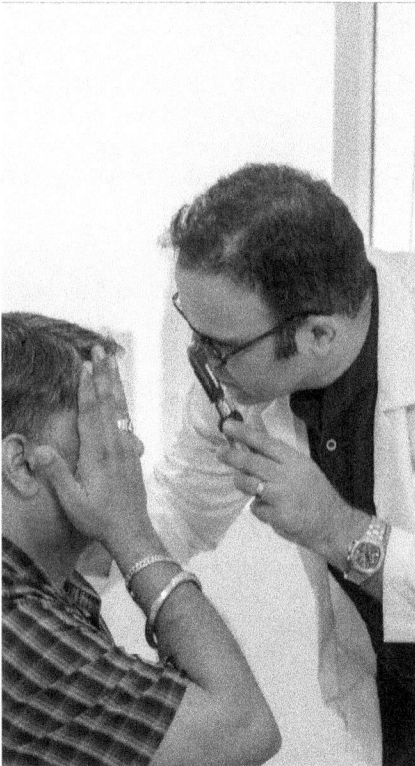

The common-sense rules for sleep hygiene include;

Creating a restful bedroom environment, in a quiet, dark room with a comfortable temperature. Avoid watching TV or using any electronic devices before going to bed, as they can stimulate your brain for several hours after use, which makes the act of falling asleep difficult.

Stimulants such as caffeine can take up to six hours to wear off, so avoid coffee, chocolate or any other stimulant after 6 pm. On the other end of the spectrum is alcohol, which can make you drowsy. Yet whilst this may help you fall asleep initially, the length and quality will be heavily impacted.

Don't eat a heavy meal before going to sleep, as your digestive system will be forced to work when it should be resting. A light meal is best, as being hungry will also disturb your sleep.

Exercise regularly during the day to help you have a better night's sleep, but avoid vigorous exercise three hours before going to bed. Relaxing exercises like yoga are best before bed.

Getting regular exposure to natural light, like morning and early afternoon light, will help you to maintain a healthy sleep-wake cycle.

Create a relaxing bedtime routine. When you are stressed or anxious, your body produces more cortisol (the stress hormone), so give yourself time to wind down before going to sleep. Try meditating or having a warm bath before going to bed.

Limit or avoid taking long naps during the day, as this will affect the quality of your nighttime sleep.

SLEEPING IN THE MIDDLE EAST

Sleep apnoea and hyperpnoea syndrome, is brought about by being overweight with a poor diet, and physical inactivity, and is prevalent in the Middle East. Dr Nami's research indicates a direct correlation between BMI and sleep issues, and worryingly has found that unhealthy lifestyle habits in younger generations have directly affected their sleep today. Smoking, fast food, poor sleep hygiene, and increased screen-time, all play their part in the rising prevalence of sleep disorders.

At the BrainHub Polyclinic, Dr Nami and his colleagues study "intermittent hypoxia during sleep and its impact on memory, attention, productivity, and mood. "Building upon his findings and those of other experts, it turns out that in a community like Dubai, 20-25% of the middle-aged population suffer from some degree of breathing

disorder during sleep, which directly affects the oxygen levels. Contrary to popular belief, snoring is not a sign of a good or deep sleep; it's a "clinical red flag." Snoring is caused mostly by the narrowing of the upper-airway, which results in "intermittent drops in the oxygen level." This is shown to cause not only brain-related dysfunctions but also conditions such as hypertension, diabetes, obesity and many other health issues.

THE BRAINHUB POLYCLINIC

Elham Bazireh (Entrepreneur, CEO at BrainHub) and Mohammad Nami are the co-founders of the Brainhub Polyclinic. With their shared initiative and collective efforts, the BrainHub Polyclinic is now geared up to raise awareness of the importance of sleep and brain health. "Sleep problems significantly impact the brain dynamics since our memory and emotions are consolidated, and processed during sleep, and that's perhaps what dreaming is all about." Sleep helps us to reverberate and reprocess our emotions and mood during the day. Furthermore, it affects our memory, sustained focus or concentration, hand-eye coordination, motor performance and sensory aptitude. This is owing to the fact that our brain and body get cleared-up from the waste materials during different stages of sleep.

In principle, almost all of our bodily functions have something to do with the brain, and "the brain is served, restored and repaired during sleep." He explains further, that

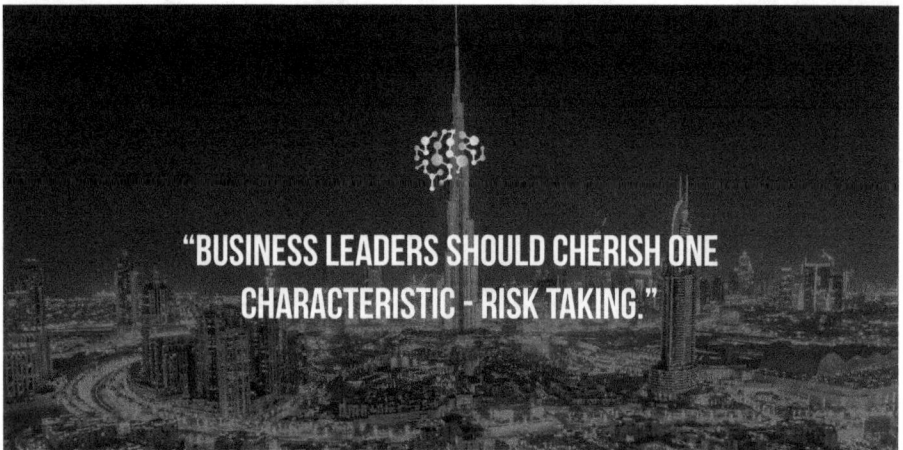

"BUSINESS LEADERS SHOULD CHERISH ONE CHARACTERISTIC - RISK TAKING."

if sleep health is not there, then general health will be impacted. Today, his practice incorporates conventional methods of sleep medicine along with focusing on the "brain side." He explains, "it's not only the airway, or the oxygen level which should be attended to. Our sleep efficiency has much to do with sleep cycle integrity as well as the sleep microstructure at the brain level." He suggests that neuro-screening, or brain checkups should be incorporated into the annual wellness checks, and brain healthcare providers need to have an even deeper look into the impact of sleep disorders on mood, cognition, motor performance, behaviour and sensory functions.

Empirical evidence confirms that getting enough quality-sleep is vital in improving cognitive ability, and supporting emotional and behavioural balance. "A good sleep will affect almost every system in your body." He warns that chronic sleep deprivation can lead to various diseases and conditions such as diabetes, hypertension, stroke or heart attack, as well as many types of cancers.

POWER NAPS

Sleeping for almost thirty minutes during the day can be of great benefit in re-energising the brain, and Dr Nami advocates for business leaders to, at some stage during the working day, close their office door, switch off their devices and take a power nap if they can. On the other hand, he also warns that napping for over half an hour during the day can negatively affect your nighttime sleep. According to him, our body and our brain are biologically hardwired to a so-called circadian clock, whereby some proteins, neurohormones and genes are specifically programmed to be active over the night hours. The circadian rhythms govern the biological changes that follow the 24-hour cycle, and studies have identified specific genes responsible for regulation of the day and night cycle. This is one reason why shift workers can suffer from certain disorders if their night work regularly lasts for more than four hours at a time. This issue has been taken up in industry, where work patterns are changed so that employees are not continuously working at night.

EGO

As an esteemed neuroscientist and successful entrepreneur, Dr Nami proposes that "we step outside our ego and serve in a genuine way to provide value to people, raise awareness, share insights with others and help others grow to be a thriving part of communities."

For him, connection is paramount, and his shared works with the Society for Brain Mapping and Therapeutics, the Canadian University in Dubai, as well as his leadership role at the BrainHub Polyclinic are testaments to his passion for networking, connecting, collaborating and creating working-teams. His desire to expand networks has also supported his philanthropic endeavours and "nobler motives." For example, for the past eight years, Dr Nami has contributed towards Brain Awareness Week, striving for the regional and global recognition of the importance of brain health. He has also been part of the World Health Innovation Summit Initiatives, Davos Alzheimer's Initiative, Senses Cultural Foundation, and Inclusive Brain Health (Swiss Alternative Medicine), as well as the Breathe Initiative through the Global Wellness Institute.

SCALING-UP

Dr Nami suggests that entrepreneurs and business leaders need to pursue ways to empower their brain-based capacity, level-max their cognitive and behavioural health, and maintain their sleep health. When it's time to scale-up, luck and timing are both great stepping stones, but we can succeed without relying on them. We shall trust the process, and the people who are with us on our journey. As Dr Nami and his colleagues aim to scale the BrainHub Polyclinic up, he will be sure to take his own counsel. "We are going to embrace this adventure, and we are very confident that this will bring value. Once you bring true value to people, you remain credible, then visible, and that's where the professional outcomes will follow. Like most other growing startups, we started with the pre-seed, seed, series a, and extended to series b plans. Today, we remain disciplined and focused, and decisively follow up with our mission statement at BrainHub which is becoming a centre of excellence for Brain Health-related services in Dubai."

DUBAI
BUSINESS
LEADERS

SENEM ANATACA

FOUNDER & CEO OF 18OUTC

"In a world filled with noise, constant change and expectations, make your choices in accordance with your core values and your vision. Every choice comes with advantages and disadvantages, but staying true to yourself and your vision makes disadvantages bearable. Sometimes it may require you to make bold decisions, and you may even find that most of your loved ones (or team members) are against your choice, but remember that it is your vision, and you only live life once. Embrace your unique journey and let it resonate with you."

MARIUS BOGDAN PISLARIU

'Billionaires' Broker' in Driven Arabia,
TOP 20 Realtors to Watch Out For in 2023, 30 Dubai's Business Leaders
Recommended by HNWI & UHNWI across the world

Above all else, Marius describes himself as a human, an inventor, and an entrepreneur. Yet, his endeavours and accomplishments extend so much further, into the worlds of consulting, public speaking, authorship, and real estate. It's no surprise, then, that at 42 years old he considers himself to have lived two lives. Originally from Romania, he has two degrees, one in Industrial and Product Design and another in PR, Advertising and Communication. He lived in Tokyo for seven years, has been involved in nine NGOs, and has been the recipient of countless awards for his inventions. Since 2018, he has been selling property in Dubai, and has recently been voted "Top 20 Realtors to look out for in 2023."

Despite having already lived such a full life, Marius is very conscious of just how precious time is and advises to "never put your life on hold for anything or anyone because it's too precious." He suggests that personal relationships are a "sacrifice," which is "not justified because you have to be loyal to yourself." Prioritising being "loyal" to himself has clearly paid off if his Instagram is anything to go by, displaying an aspirational life filled with glamour and opulence. Yet, the journey hasn't been easy, and external circumstances have sometimes delayed his ambitions. In 2017, he already had his sights set on Dubai, but the diplomatic crisis in Qatar diverted him from Tokyo back to his home country, Romania. However, when one door shuts, another opens, and in 2018, Marius won first place in Europe's 'Best Local Economic Development Programme'.

"START YOUNG, YOUTH IS THE BATTLEFIELD FOR FAILURE AND LEARNING, AND THAT IS MAGNIFICENT."

EVERYONE'S HEADING FOR DUBAI

One day, out of the blue, Marius received a call from his mentor and friend of 30 years, who was based in Dubai at the time. He said, "Marius, the market is improving, I'm coming to pick you up in three days, get ready." So, in 2018, he packed up, moved to Dubai, and has never looked back. In 2022, he launched a real estate platform. "It revolutionises the property buying experience in Dubai with a constantly updated inventory." It's user-friendly and buyer focused, featuring live prices, updated availability, and comparisons.

There are times when Marius craves the cool climate and lush, verdant landscapes of his beloved Romania. "I miss forests and mountains, so travelling to my home country helps me." Nevertheless, there are plenty of people around the globe who view Dubai as their dream destination, whether it's for work, holidays, or simply to live.

He observes that "people really want to move and live here" and views being a realtor as more of a lifestyle than a 9-5 job, as he'll often answer calls at 2am from people around the globe enquiring about his properties. He manages this by "working smarter," using a template to personalise property searches. This means that clients will receive automated notifications when a potential match arrives on the market, saving "something like 80% of the broker's time and also increasing the chances to sell."

Marius suggests that Dubai is "on the lips of every high net worth individual and ultra-net worth individual in the world." Safety seems to be the number one reason for this recent surge in interest, and as a resident himself, he can personally attest to the lack of crime, robberies, paparazzi, and vandalism.

SOLID ADVICE

Despite his praise of Dubai, he also warns against "brokers and agents who have come for the gold rush and the dream of making easy money, spreading misleading information, and using pushing strategies" to sell properties. Marius is keen to point out what differentiates him and his team is the value system and personal connection with a real interest in the customer. He basically provides a "buyer advisory service," where he is not afraid to tell customers the truth about certain projects and "the fact that they will not have the income that they are hoping for, or the appreciation or profitability that they are expecting." He warns that in real estate, some agents will lie to get the commission, and customers will buy into it because "they want to believe in a dream."

Marius also advises "moving here for at least 6 months to really understand how things work and how the market is operating," particularly as an entrepreneur. While he admires those who come to Dubai and "have the guts to open a company straight away without investigating the market," he suggests researching the market in the US, Europe, and Japan first before making any decisions.

THE BOOK LOVER

There were times when Marius didn't have much money, and the little he did have was used "for bus tickets and for books." So as a self-confessed bibliophile, Marius has a couple of books to recommend for anyone looking to change their outlook and reach their goals. Og Mandino's 'The Greatest Salesperson in the World' is a personal favourite and has a prescriptive reading format telling a simple storyline of a poor boy who gained great wealth. He also recommends another book by his friend Rafael Badziag, 'The Billion Dollar Secret' which helped him completely "shift [his] mindset." It impacted him so deeply that he ordered 200 copies to hand out.

SCIENCE FICTION TO SCIENCE FACT

Although Marius believes that "AI is changing the world as we speak, and we still don't know if it will be for the better or worse," he is nevertheless of the opinion that the education system in general needs a "revolution", so that it becomes accessible to everyone. He believes this is something that AI "could play a major role in because it can generate a personalised education system according to the needs and way of thinking of every single individual."

He looks forward to a time when "intellectual industrial property" is no longer protected, but instead "will be used for the common good of everyone so that we can exponentially grow." He references "open-source codes" as an example of how intellectual property can benefit individuals as opposed to companies.

INVENTOR AND VISIONARY

As a young boy, Marius was forever disassembling things to investigate how they worked, from his sister's toy doll to his father's wristwatch. Decades later, he has amassed an eclectic and highly imaginative list of inventions, which range from a greenhouse heated by waste heat to a sensor cane for the blind, a monowheel electric mobility vehicle, a bed that rises to the ceiling and perfumed jewellery. However, he points to a well-known saying among inventors, "The best invention is not the one that was created yesterday, not the one created today, but the one that is created tomorrow." In other words, as an inventor, you must always "innovate and come up with new solutions, new technologies, and new things to help customers."

When Marius invents, he feels as if he is actually creating, and it's like "being connected with higher intelligence, and this brings [him] so much joy, peace, and energy." He also considers inventing an almost spiritual process. "Sometimes, I just need to sleep for 10 minutes to find the solution to a problem, and in those 10 minutes, I can actually feel my rapid eye movement, then I wake up and have the solution."

Like many people at the forefront of technology and future developments, Marius warns against AI and customer confidence, "I think the industry will be affected by how automated building machines deliver, it might happen for low-rise buildings, but skyscrapers are a totally different story."

SECRETS OF A SUCCESSFUL LEADER

Marius suggests that people often view success through the eyes of profit, but believes there isn't a definition wide enough to define success. He explains that we all emerge from different backgrounds with a different set of values and questions whether "the positive revenue of a business" should be valued above the "sacrifice of a single parent raising a functional, kind human being."

As a prosperous businessman and leader, he argues that the success and happiness of his employees and clients are just as important as "financial strength, status, market reach and time coverage." Proposing that the main purpose of a leader, "beyond breathing integrity," is to ensure that everyone shares their vision. "Success is not just about money, it's more about how many quality people are willing to follow a leader, join in the company's values, and turn it to the benefit of the customers. Once ignited, these conditions will bring extremely satisfied customers and profits will undoubtedly follow."

Beyond that, Marius has flexible working arrangements for his employees, giving them the freedom to work when and where they choose as long as they are transparent and self-disciplined. "Automated operations allow for maximum flexibility on time and location, a transparent hierarchy, a bonus scheme built on individual achievement and a supportive leader." For Marius, part of being a successful leader is the ability to "recognise willing team players," and for those who rise to the challenge, he ensures they are rewarded.

ADVICE FOR ENTREPRENEURS

As the founder of several businesses and nurturing a few franchises, Marius shares his wisdom for others wishing to start their own enterprise. "Consider gathering a good team, set up a system that will run even when you are not around, keep your eyes and ears open as the people you interact with are pointing you in the right direction." Ensure your product or service will serve the market well and use online marketing tools to promote it. His other nuggets include:

- The Pareto principle - 20% of your customers bring 80% of the revenue.

- Invest in yourself and your team: you absolutely deserve the best and if you wish to keep that front-row seat, then your profit is worth reinvesting.

- Keep yourself informed about the technology, software, courses, workshops, people and do not cut corners. It will pay off in the end.

- Online marketing is a gold mine - you can reach millions with just one click.

- Create pockets for the company expenses and allocate a budget for unseen circumstances.

- Keep a healthy cash flow close to you. A couple of months ahead is good, a year in advance even better.

MULTIFACETED

Marius' social media profile presents a man who likes his cigars, fine wines, tailored suits, luxurious settings, and expensive cars. However, there is so much more than meets the eye. It's difficult to define a man who sells luxury property to multimillionaires while being able to quote Albert Camus and William Shakespeare. As a prolific inventor, he has had three patents granted by the State Office for Patents and Trademarks, and 50 other inventions under patent. As an entrepreneur, he has founded a number of successful companies, and as a human, he "is the sum of all [his] dreams and desires." With all this life experience under his belt, Marius is a multifaceted man with a unique perspective on the world. As an inventor, successful entrepreneur, purveyor of splendour, and simple bookworm, he has rolled a multitude of lives into one, and there is still more to come.

"STAY HUMBLE, AT ANY GIVEN POINT, AND KEEP AN OPEN EYE TOWARDS RISKS, COSTS, TIME AND COMPETITION."

DUBAI
BUSINESS
LEADERS

"The power of networking is the most important skill that you need to develop."

Leena Pareena
Founder and Investor

"I have come to understand through the process of collecting Nuggets that storms come not to blow us off course, but to clear our path forward"

Steven Foster
Founder and CEO - One Golden Nugget

SILVIA MOGAS

CEO & Founder of Blockchain Marketing Boutique &
Verify Trust, Women of the future TOP100, International
Speaker, Lecturer, Advisor & Mentor Executive MBA

A s a marketing and blockchain enthusiast, Silvia has managed to incorporate both of her passions into a number of enterprises. The exponential growth of technology has offered her the opportunity to become what she is now, CEO of Blockchain Boutique Marketing, and she has been recognised as one of the Top Women of the Future in Emerging Tech for 2023 and Top Marketing Strategy Voice by LinkedIn. Her tech-based company guides businesses in their inevitable transition to Web3.0, by building marketing strategies that support growth and sustainability in this new era towards a better and more decentralised internet.

Staying with her affinity for technological innovation, and marketing experience, Silvia's most recent project is a start-up, aptly named 'Verify Trust'. The SaaS pioneering ecosystem is a marketing tool that will help their customers to receive feedback on their products and services.

"COLLABORATION IS THE MAIN PATH TOWARDS GROWTH."

Silvia's career path could be considered both a long journey and a whirlwind. With so much work experience, and qualifications, Silvia has moved from managerial positions in marketing, to being the founder and CEO of two tech-based companies, as well as an advisor, mentor and judge at Stanford AI & Web3.0 Research Lab Association, R3 Corda, and SBC Inclusive Fintech & DeFi Program. She lectures about Web3.0, AI, innovation and marketing, and also she is a global speaker. This year she has participated in events in Dubai, Romania, Austria, Estonia, Switzerland, Andorra, Spain, the UK, France and Portugal, and she has also mentored more than 20 startups.

Although marketing and blockchain technology could be viewed as her two main interests, Silvia has also found time to enjoy activities which have taken her far away from the office and computer. The Web3 enthusiast likes to get back to nature and enjoys horse-riding and trekking, as well as spending time with her dog, Lola, and her friends. But for the most part, her work is her life, and it's what makes Silvia who she is; curious, resilient and adventurous, with an uncompromising desire to help improve the world.

THE FUTURE

Silvia considers her postgraduate diploma, MBA, and other numerous qualifications as an investment. She has climbed the ladder of success one rung at a time, and has quickly established herself as an important player in the Web3 and Blockchain space.

She admits that, although there are more women coming into the sector, it's still very much a male-dominated space. As an industry leader and educator for AllWomen, a learning platform directed at women in tech, Silvia advises that "you have to be able to have your voice in the middle of twenty men." She's also keen to point out that regardless of the pitfalls, there are countless rewards, and as an ardent technologist, Silvia believes Web3 and blockchain technology are "the future," and through her journey of exploration has met "an amazing community of people." For her, people are at the heart of everything that matters.

She explains, in simple terms, just why she views it as the future. Whereas Web2 relies on a centralised process, where information is stored by a few big firms, Web3 offers democratisation, and the ownership of your assets. With Web3 people no longer need to rely on intermediaries or centralised platforms to manage their assets. Instead, they can directly interact with decentralised networks and use blockchain technology to ensure transparency, security, and ownership of their digital assets. This shift towards self-ownership and decentralised control is one of the key reasons why she believes that Web3 is shaping the future of technology.

Silvia's agency has a strong focus on three verticals. The first vertical is helping Web2 brands make the transition to Web3. The agency provides expertise in strategy, technology, legal and compliance, and marketing execution, building a bridge between Web2 and Web3. This includes developing Web2.5 solutions that integrate with the Web3 ecosystem. Silvia is excited about working with clients in various sectors, including finance, travel brands, retail, art, wineries, and NGOs like others. Secondly, the agency works with native Web3 brands such as Xhype, a Dubai-based company. They are providing valuable support in international marketing and communications, helping them to reach a global audience.

The third vertical is education. Silvia and her team are building an academy to help future professionals enter the Web3 world. She recognises that education is crucial for mass adoption of Web3 technologies. The academy will provide people with the necessary skills and knowledge to work in this evolving industry. Overall, Silvia's agency is well-positioned to provide

comprehensive support for companies interested in exploring and adopting Web3 technologies.

LISTEN AND LEARN

To maintain her level of expertise and versatility, Silvia makes sure that she keeps up to date with the ever-evolving trends in the industry. As a leader, she also understands the need to "lead by example," describing an effective leader as someone interested in their people, being able to give them the right tools to do their job well, resulting in company growth and high morale. Having worked in several corners of the world, she also has a view of internationally based leaders, who she believes need "to understand the local people, their culture and be prepared to listen to them."

As a lecturer, and life-long learner, Silvia reads a lot of technology news, listens to a wide range of podcasts and attends many conferences to learn as much as she can about her industry and be able to impart the latest innovations to her students.

HR

With many years of experience in head of department roles, Silvia instinctively knows what to look for in a candidate's CV. She knows experience is probably the most important, but for Silvia, it's more about attitude. She also values education highly, and suggests you can work while still learning and gaining qualifications. She also values soft skills that are often overlooked by employers, and of course, it's important that her employees reflect her business ethos of making the world a better place; values and ethics are a must.

AI

As a speaker at AI and Web3 events, she likes to share her own experiences and informed perspectives on the constantly changing phenomenon, and feels very privileged to be part of a community with only a handful of experts. Although she loves the idea of AI helping people and businesses, and she believes it is definitely here to stay, she is also part of a growing number of experts developing reservations about the potential ramifications of AI, and encourages caution.

THE DUBAI CONNECTION

Although not officially living in Dubai, Silvia spends a lot of time there, and has a strong connection to the city through her work. She likes the way business is done through word of mouth, and notes that one of the reasons why companies choose to be located in Dubai is due to the flexibility and leniency. This was the principal motivation behind one of her clients, XHype, choosing to establish their base in Dubai.

"NEVER LET ANYONE TELL YOU THAT YOU CAN'T DO IT. BELIEVE IN YOURSELF AND GO AFTER YOUR DREAMS, NO MATTER WHAT OTHERS SAY. IF YOU STUMBLE AND FALL, RISE AGAIN AND KEEP PUSHING UNTIL YOUR DREAM BECOMES A REALITY."

With Silvia's knowledge of Web3 and blockchain, XHype can boast of being the first decentralised payment system, offering customers experiences which they can pay for using crypto. The company sought Silvia's expertise because part of their business model requires, specifically, not storing clients' data, or using intermediaries such as banks. The financial transactions at XHype are completely anonymous, in an ecosystem focusing on a fair and transparent trading platform. It's a revolution, claims Silvia.

Being "six hours from both Barcelona and Singapore" in Dubai is important for Silvia, as a native of Barcelona and having grown a base in Singapore while she lived there. In fact, Dubai is geographically central to most parts of the world, which is an added benefit for a company like XHype with a global reach. Dubai is well known for being a big player in the sphere of technology, innovation, and space exploration, so Silvia has many opportunities to network with people who have similar passions. If she can't attend events in person, virtual events are handy "to get to know people in the industry and connect with them."

A BALANCED LIFE

As a busy entrepreneur and CEO of several companies, Silvia finds it challenging to take time out to relax and unwind, believing that discipline and commitment to self are crucial to success. She finds inspiration during the night when the city quiets down and distractions are at a minimum, allowing her creativity to flourish. She also prioritises daily exercise, whether it's at the gym, horse riding, running, or practising yoga, recognising its health and mental benefits. Furthermore, Silvia values hiking with her loyal dog, Lola, and spending quality time with her friends, who she describes as her "batteries", allowing her the chance to recuperate and continue with her entrepreneurial endeavours with a fresh mind.

Silvia also makes sure that she prepares for each day the night before, believing that planning is the key to tackling the following day's challenges. She also takes the time to reflect on the day that has gone by, acknowledging the things that went well and those that did not meet her expectations. This reflection time offers a learning experience that she can use to improve on the following day and allows her the satisfaction of knowing she has done her best with the time she has each day, helping her to stay motivated and focused on achieving her goals.

A BETTER WORLD

Collaboration and balance are the two most important elements for Silvia when looking towards a brighter future. She stresses the need for "more equality of resources", where people with a lot, support those who have little. Whilst she's certainly realistic about the consumer society that has created this imbalance, she also feels optimistic about Web3's role in fostering a more even playing field. Furthermore, she's happy to talk politics, and she believes that governments should be more impartial, prioritising the best interests of society and the economy.

For Silvia, collaboration is the only way forward, where countries work together to solve issues, and people are happy to share resources. Her egalitarian ideology is clearly embedded in her interest in Web3 and the blockchain "revolution" whose purpose it is to democratise a space which some may say has been dominated for far too long, by only a few.

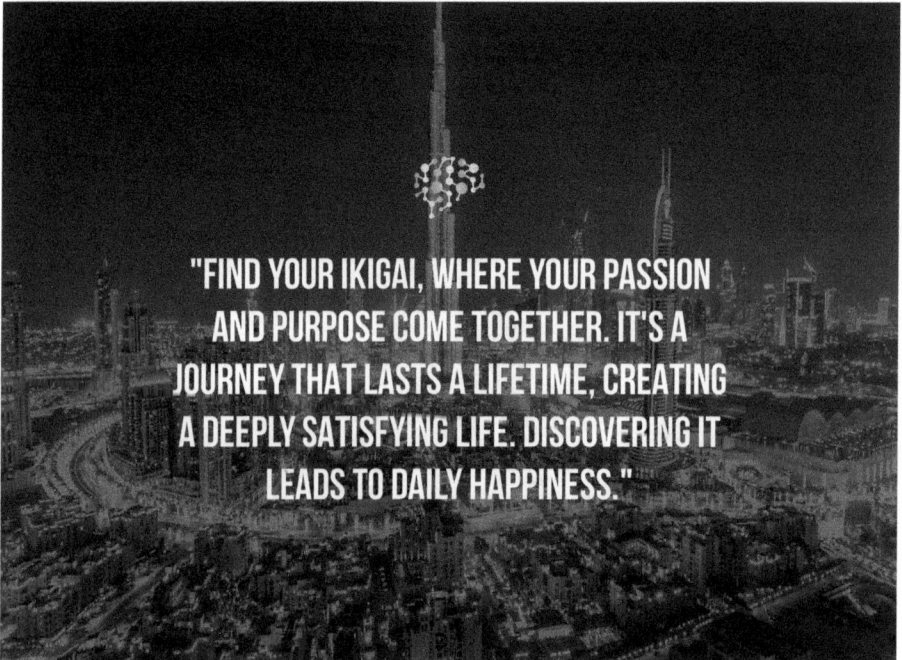

"FIND YOUR IKIGAI, WHERE YOUR PASSION AND PURPOSE COME TOGETHER. IT'S A JOURNEY THAT LASTS A LIFETIME, CREATING A DEEPLY SATISFYING LIFE. DISCOVERING IT LEADS TO DAILY HAPPINESS."

DUBAI
BUSINESS
LEADERS

VYARA TOSHEVA

Business Manager at RESYNC, Wellness Consultancy
and Coaching Founder at Vybe Management,
Twice-Published Author and Entrepreneur

V yara's purpose in life is to seek the truth in her spiritual journey and help others to explore their inner truths, not just by following gurus or reading books, but by delving into themselves on a much deeper level. She describes herself as "the Vybewoman" whose mission is to "raise the vibes of others" as she is convinced that "keeping a good state of mind requires firstly self-maintenance and discipline."

For Vyara, an essential part of keeping a good state of mind is always to follow your passion and instincts and continue to challenge yourself when something doesn't feel right. In Vyara's case, it was satisfying her curiosity by leaving her home country at the age of 19 years old to explore the world. Originally from Bulgaria, Vyara holds a degree in Tourism and Travel and a Masters in Psychology and Sociology of Management. She speaks four languages, volunteers as a World Wellness Weekend Ambassador for the UAE to help people harness the power of wellness, and has worked as a Reiki therapist for cancer survivors.

Vyara has benefited from "many spiritual teachers, humans and people" who she believes, have been in her life for a reason and contributed to who she is today. Nevertheless, she's certain that "the best treasure lies in oneself." It's taken time for Vyara to find that truth, and she speaks candidly about her spiritual journey. She

"DON'T ALLOW ROUTINES TO DICTATE YOU, YOU DICTATE THE ROUTINES."

confesses to having been "born with a massive ego" and puts it partially down to the collective unconscious of the Balkan region she was born in. Therefore, an essential part of her journey has been discovering that behind the ego, in fact, "hides the biggest truth and potential." When she could separate from it, she "happened to realise that [her] ego was based on nothing but empty chatter, needing reassurance and peace. Vyara has had repeating journeys of being left with nothing, no money, no resources, no friends, or family."

Vyara's journey from being left without money and a home, during the pandemic, to building and running two successful businesses is an inspiring story of resilience, determination, and adaptability. She had to overcome adversity and acknowledge her situation, when she hit rock-bottom of having only $100 in her pocket and no place to live. At that breaking point, she "committed to use it as a starting point for her comeback." She relentlessly took advantage of online courses, webinars, and free resources to acquire the necessary knowledge in e-commerce, online education and training in health and wellness.

She actively reached out to her professional contacts and joined online communities related to her chosen field, and started working in low-paying jobs just to cover her monthly expenses. With limited funds, Vyara had to be frugal. She created a detailed budget, cutting unnecessary expenses, and working long hours to keep the door of her wellness consultancy open. This "financial and lifestyle discipline allowed [her] to make a living while seeking resources for bootstrapping her business.

Vyara maintained a positive and resilient mindset and had a commitment to self-improvement and adaptability. She understood that set backs were part of entrepreneurship and used them as opportunities to learn and grow.

Yet, her faith and ability to maintain inner peace despite despicable adversity have allowed her to reframe these experiences as "beautiful journeys." Today, as she runs two businesses, one being a high-tech longevity studio and another being her wellness coaching and consulting practice, she can reflect on her journey to see how far she's come.

BECOMING VYARA

When she was 20 years old, Vyara became interested in combining "experiences with a retreating lifestyle," so she learned everything she could on creating exceptional wellness retreats and ventured on a journey creating "New Life" retreat experiences for famous tour operators such as Neckerman and Thomas Cook. Initially, things weren't smooth sailing, and she felt she had "failed many times." Sometimes by not having enough budget for ideas implementation, sometimes by consumers and business operators not being very open to modalities and experiences, however, always the optimist, she believed that these "only helped [her] to learn faster."

The low times were there to "shrink down [her] ego and get [her] to really understand who [she] was at that point." She was also aware that this experience and inner journey were helping her to understand "what [she] could truly do with [her] own potential and power on the mission she has in this life." Of course, Vyara knew that she needed a "support mechanism" to contribute to the business; it was not something she could do herself.

Having managed small and big teams in leisure and wellness outlets, she considers herself "the coordinator rather than the boss." It's a simple strategy, as she explains, "you just make sure that you coordinate correctly for people to perform their tasks smoothly and empower them to feel in charge."

VYBE MANAGEMENT AND VYBEWOMAN:

Now a leading figure in Dubai's growing wellness industry, Vyara extends her expertise to help others build their businesses. She has always believed in her ability to "influence and impact people in terms of their state of mind," she starts with understanding

people on a "human level," looking at what motivates them and helping them in finding their purpose.

Once this has been established, she can "build them up." Vyara established her coaching and consulting practice Vybe Management in 2014, initially well-known as the "Vybewoman" and later branched into a Vybe Management for her business. As a wellness consultancy providing support and guidance to businesses and start-ups, it's all about nurturing a wellbeing environment that encourages professional growth by offering personalised management services, career development and strategic planning. Vybe Management aims to tackle specific business stages; incubation, growth and monetisation. By offering wellness

coaching, business consultation, and workshops, Vybe Management aims to promote sustainability and accelerated growth for the businesses it collaborates with.

LONGEVITY THROUGH BIOHACKING

Although Vyara is successful at helping others achieve their own business goals, nowadays, her passion expands over "achieving longevity through biohacking." In her sector, this involves red light, cryotherapy hydrogen and oxygen therapy. According to Vyara, these therapies are based on scientific research from NASA, which found that human cells are reproduced and regenerated through light, cold and hot technologies. Hence, for space exploration, this is something that needs to be produced artificially, NASA apparently experimented with frequencies, wavelengths, vibrations, penetrating noninvasively into the skin, reaching the bones and muscle levels. Blood circulation is stimulated at this point, which distributes nutrients and "basically repairs, heals, and stimulates the collagen production which helps your cells to rejuvenate, recover and reproduce."

DISCOVERING VYARA

Approaching her twenties, Vyara already started asking herself the big life questions, "why am I here, what is my purpose, and what should I accomplish before I leave." This sense of self-exploration and desire for truth and understanding prompted Vyara to start writing diaries, small publications for school magazines and also appear in her school production. During the pandemic, she diverted this passion toward writing her first book and started collaboration with UAE magazines and online publications.

"BY SEEKING YOUR DEEP-ROOTED TRUTH, YOU INSTANTLY HELP OTHERS SHINE THE LIGHT ON THEIRS."

Having written as a child, she considers this venture a "path of rediscovering [herself] and satisfying [her] own seeker's journey."

In her first book, 'Who Moved My Heels', Vyara shares her journey from misery to mastery during the pandemic, from being broke and penniless to being again in charge of her life. Her second book, 'DIY Wellness at Hotels and Spas', was published without fanfare or marketing strategies, and she hopes that word of mouth will connect her story with the right people.

Vyara suggests driving sales in Dubai is a two-pronged system. Although rapid technological development is imperative for any modern business, especially in Dubai, where technological innovation is embraced, what clinches the sale is "the relationship, true, authentic, genuine, unapologetic, sometimes heart-grown relationships." She suggests, "you need to be true to yourself first, then true to the person you serve." Vyara quickly notices that "everything happening in Dubai recently has the metaverse version. Even spiritual gurus have created a kind of metaverse experience where people can participate in a virtual retreat from the comfort of their homes." Health trackers have also become a major wellness gadget, as they can monitor oxygen and hormone levels, sleep routines and much more. Vyara envisions that technology will be more central in most aspects of our lives.

Her motivation is dependent on "how much [she] can deliver wellness and wellbeing to [herself] first, and then influence others." She believes that "as long as you are open and embrace everything that the time and space offers you, and as long as you are adaptable to drive on that new technology or new trends that are happening or evolving, you will succeed in your business." Whilst there are instances that require extensive long-term plans in business, Vyara suggests that on a larger scale, adaptability and having a flexible, out of the box thinking helps a lot in a city like Dubai because of the "ever-changing dynamics, you wake up and there is a new rule or regulation."

IT'S IN YOUR DNA

Vyara suggests that "success comes about when you are genuine, true to yourself, and so the questions and answers are always in you." She advises that regardless of how many teachers, gurus or mentors there are, "you have to figure it out yourself." She sees business as "an extension of your life, therefore, you need to be genuine. If you open a business just because it's on trend, or someone says how popular it is, it will fail." She proposes that you need to make your business part of your DNA to succeed; it must be part of "your map of the world". She observes that "most of us are driving on autopilot 95% of the time, driven by our subconsciousness. For that reason,

we rarely have that insight to question ourselves." Truth Seeker Vyara suggests that "routines are creating habits and habits are creating a consistency or a set of rules you follow in your life." She explains, "I don't allow the routines to dictate me; I dictate the routines."

She lives intuitively and listens to her body and her mind. For example, one morning, she might wake up with enough energy to run 5 km, whilst another morning, she may feel she only wants to incorporate some stretch routines and slow-paced activities. She suggests that "you should allow yourself to listen to your body rather than saying to yourself I have a routine I have to follow."

Her life's philosophy is all about seeking truth. "Life is all about happenings of pain and pleasure, a series of lessons that offer you wisdom." For Vyara, it's up to each individual to accept these lessons and transform themselves, or ignore them and have a life of "self-pity, self-sabotage, regret and blame." Her advice is to "go back to the beginning; it's about your personal DNA, how you internalise, reflect and transform," but it's also about being authentic, genuine and true to yourself.

Over time, Vyara's dedication, adaptability, and hard work paid off. Her business not only survived the pandemic, but also thrived, becoming a symbol of resilience and success in the face of adversity. Her story serves as an inspiration to others facing similar challenges, showing that with determination and the right strategies, it's possible to turn adversity into an opportunity for growth and success.

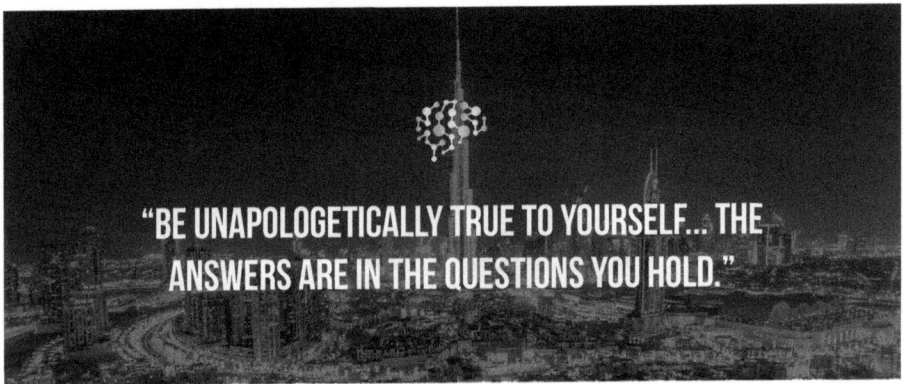

"BE UNAPOLOGETICALLY TRUE TO YOURSELF... THE ANSWERS ARE IN THE QUESTIONS YOU HOLD."

ROHIT RAJASEKHARAN

CHIEF TRANSFORMATION OFFICER
OF LATO MILK

"Your net worth is your network. Whether it's personal or professional, your connections with people will enrich every experience you have in life. To be able to connect with people, share ideas, learn and inspire each other will bring you joy. So surround yourself with people who help you grow and develop that winning mindset."

GRATITUDE

We would like to thank everyone who has generously shared their one golden nugget of wisdom. Their support and thoughtful words have helped build this extraordinary movement and create connections around the world. And to our amazing co-authors who have believed and trusted in us to tell their stories - we are grateful.

DO YOU HAVE A STORY TO TELL?

WWW.DUBAIBUSINESSLEADERS.COM

www.ingramcontent.com/pod-product-compliance
Lightning Source LLC
Chambersburg PA
CBHW071537200326
41519CB00021BB/6520